T0226676

Pattern Recognition
in Industry

Pattern Recognition
in Industry

Phiroz Bhagat

International Strategy Engines
New Jersey, USA

2005

ELSEVIER

Amsterdam – Boston – Heidelberg – London – New York – Oxford – Paris
San Diego – San Francisco – Singapore – Sydney – Tokyo

ELSEVIER B.V.
Radarweg 29
P.O. Box 211, 1000 AE Amsterdam
The Netherlands

ELSEVIER Inc.
525 B Street, Suite 1900
San Diego, CA 92101-4495
USA

ELSEVIER Ltd
The Boulevard, Langford Lane
Kidlington, Oxford OX5 1GB
UK

ELSEVIER Ltd
84 Theobalds Road
London WC1X 8RR
UK

First edition 2005

Library of Congress Cataloging in Publication Data
A catalog record is available from the Library of Congress.

British Library Cataloguing in Publication Data
A catalogue record is available from the British Library.

ISBN: 0 08 044538 1

Printed and bound in the United Kingdom
Transferred to Digital Print 2009

Working together to grow
libraries in developing countries

www.elsevier.com | www.bookaid.org | www.sabre.org

ELSEVIER   BOOK AID
             International   Sabre Foundation

To my wife, Patti, and daughters, Kay and Sarah, who are *my raisons d'être*. Were it not for them, recognizing patterns would have little meaning for me.

Preface

Two wave fronts are upon us today: we are being deluged by an enormous amount of data, and we are confronted by ever increasing technical and business advances.

Ideally, the endless flow of data should be one of our major assets. However, this potential asset often tends to overwhelm rather than enrich. Competitive advantage depends on the ability to extract and utilize nuggets of valuable knowledge and insight from this data deluge. The challenges that need to be overcome include the under-utilization of available data due to competing priorities, and the separate and somewhat disparate existing data systems that have difficulty interacting with each other.

Technical and business fronts are advancing exponentially. The growing number of new processes to be comprehended and controlled, and the increasing levels of detail and complexity to be mastered in order to satisfy market forces call for capturing and assimilating knowledge through novel modeling techniques. Conventional approaches to formulating models are often inadequate given today's intense time and cost pressures. To impart a competitive edge, engineering[1] science as deployed in industry in the 21st century needs to augment (and in some cases, leapfrog) traditional modeling processes by developing models directly from operating data. Such models can be easily updated as fresh data become available so as to reflect changing conditions. This approach has wide applicability; in areas ranging from manufacturing processes, product performance and scientific research, to financial and business fields.

This book explores pattern recognition technology, and its concomitant role in extracting useful knowledge to build technical and business models directly from data, and in optimizing the results derived from these models within the context of delivering competitive industrial advantage. It is not intended to serve as a comprehensive reference source on the subject. Rather, it is based on first-hand experience in the practice of this technology: its development and deployment for profitable application in industry. The technical topics in the book will focus on the triad of technological areas that constitute the contemporary workhorses of successful industrial application of pattern recognition. These are: (i) systems for self-organizing data; (ii) data-driven modeling; and (iii) genetic algorithms as robust optimizers.

---

[1]The word "engineering" comes from the Latin word *ingeniare*, which means to devise. From this we derive "ingenuity", which means inventiveness. Therefore, engineering science should, based on its etymology, be taken to mean the process of harnessing our ingenuity to the solution of problems.

This book shows how pattern recognition technology can be used to realize competitive advantage. It consists of three parts:

- Part I is an exposition of the philosophy and foundation on which pattern recognition technology is based.
- Part II is the "technical blueprint" counterpart to Part I, in which methodology, algorithms and theories are discussed.
- Part III demonstrates, through case studies, the effectiveness of the technology in solving technical and business problems.

This book serves a wide audience ranging from engineers and plant managers, business strategists and consultants, and financial analysts, to product developers and R&D managers. It will also work well as a text for an interdisciplinary course within engineering and business schools. Managers who are keen on assessing the feasibility of Pattern Recognition as a vehicle of problem solving, but not necessarily interested in the technical details, would find Parts I and III on the underlying philosophy and case studies of greatest interest.

It is my hope that this book helps widen the understanding and implementation of its approach through which profitable operating decisions are made possible by developing models directly from operating data. This new way of solving engineering and business problems should help meet the relentless demand we all feel for increasing our effectiveness in utilizing physical and information assets, and in accelerating innovation.

Phiroz Bhagat
New Jersey, USA

Acknowledgments

I am deeply grateful to my business partner, Dwarka Mimani, for his wisdom and judgment that guides our company. His copious suggestions have enhanced this monograph. The chapters on case studies in Part III have benefited very significantly from his insight and experience.

I also wish to thank my many colleagues, collaborators, and clients whose contributions have led to the development and deployment of the technology that constitutes the contents of this monograph. Special thanks to Bill Heard, my mathematical guide; and to Barry Tarmy and Bob Koros whose invaluable support enabled me to embark on my pattern recognition adventure.

Of several very great teachers that I have been fortunate to have had in my formative years, I would like to acknowledge two professors who have been especially significant in launching my professional explorations: Richard Sonntag for inspiring a passion for thermodynamics; and the late Howard Emmons for exemplifying a level of clarity and rigor in engineering understanding to which I have aspired but have yet to reach.

Most importantly, this book would not have been possible without the help and encouragement of my publisher, Henri van Dorssen. His gracious style and gentlemanly manner made our interactions most pleasurable for me.

About the Author

Phiroz Bhagat pioneered the development and application of pattern recognition technology for technical and business operations in the petroleum and chemical industry. He has developed and deployed state-of-the-art architectures. He brings to bear over two decades of experience in the application of cutting-edge technology for improved profitability and performance.

Bhagat graduated from the Indian Institute of Technology in Bombay, and earned his doctorate at the University of Michigan, Ann Arbor. He was a post-doctoral Research Fellow at Harvard University in Cambridge, Massachusetts, and then taught thermodynamics and energy conversion as a faculty member at Columbia University in New York City. After consulting with Exxon Research & Engineering Company, he joined Exxon (now ExxonMobil) in 1981. There he spearheaded major projects involving modeling and simulation of petroleum refining and chemical processes, consulting and leading investigations, enabling breakthrough designs and operational improvement of multi-million dollar plant units. His work in pattern recognition technology began in the late 1980s, and continues today. In January 2004 he co-founded International Strategy Engines, focusing on providing clients with cutting-edge pattern recognition-based solutions for improved operations and profitability. He can be reached at pmbhagat@strategyengines.com.

Contents

Preface vii

Acknowledgments ix

About the Author xi

Part I Philosophy

CHAPTER 1
INTRODUCTION

1.1. Distinguishing Knowledge and Information from Data 3

1.2. Whence Pattern Recognition Technology 4

1.3. Thermodynamic Concept of Order Leading to Information Theory 5

1.4. Modeling Informed by Observation 6

1.5. Pattern Recognition Technology Triad 7

References 8

CHAPTER 2
PATTERNS WITHIN DATA

2.1. Types of Data 9

2.2. Characterizing Data 9

2.3. Distance Between Data 11

 2.3.1 Binary Data 11

 2.3.2 Numerical Data 11

 2.3.3 Discrete or Digital Data 12

 2.3.4 Textual Data 13

2.4. Organizing Data — Clustering / Auto-Classification 13

2.5. Organizing Data — Data Series Resonance 14

2.6. Organizing Data — Correlative Modeling 14

References 15

CHAPTER 3
ADAPTING BIOLOGICAL PRINCIPLES FOR DEPLOYMENT
IN COMPUTATIONAL SCIENCE

3.1. Learning Organisms — An Introduction to Neural Nets 17

3.2. Supervised Learning 19

3.3. Unsupervised Learning 21

3.4.   Models that Self-Organize Data (Unsupervised Learning) as well as
       Correlate them with Dependent Outcomes (Supervised Learning)   22
3.5.   Genetic Algorithms   24
References   25

CHAPTER 4
ISSUES IN PREDICTIVE EMPIRICAL MODELING
4.1.   Pre-Conditioning Data: Pre- and Post-Processing   27
4.2.   Detecting Extrapolative Conditions   28
4.3.   Embedding Mechanistic Understanding / Experiential Judgment
       to Enhance Extrapolative Robustness   28
4.4.   Insight into Model Behavior   29

Part II   Technology

CHAPTER 5
SUPERVISED LEARNING — CORRELATIVE NEURAL NETS
5.1.   Supervised Learning with Back-Propagation Neural Nets   33
5.2.   Feedforward — Exercising the BP Net in Predictive Mode—Neuron
        Transformation Function   33
5.3.   BP Training — Connection Weights Adjusted by the "Delta Rule" to
        Minimize Learning Errors   36
5.4.   Back-Propagation Equations for General Transformation Functions   37
5.5.   Back-Propagation Equations for Sigmoidal Transformation Functions 39
5.6.   Conjugate Gradient Methodology for Rapid and Robust Convergence   40
5.7.   Separating Signal from Noise in Training   41
5.8.   Pre-Conditioning Data for BP Nets   42
5.9.   Supervised Learning with Radial Basis Function Neural Nets   44
5.10.   Seeding the Input Data Space with RBF Cluster Centers   44
5.11.   Assigning Spheres of Influence to each Cluster   46
5.12.   Activating Clusters from a Point in the Data Space   46
5.13.   Developing RBF Correlation Models — Assigning Weights
        to Map Outcome   47
5.14.   Pre-Conditioning Data for RBF Nets   47
5.15.   Neural Net Correlation Models   47
References   48

CHAPTER 6
UNSUPERVISED LEARNING: AUTO-CLUSTERING AND
SELF-ORGANIZING DATA
6.1. Unsupervised Learning — Value to Industry   49
6.2. Auto-Clustering Using Radial Basis Functions   49
6.3. RBF Cluster Radius   50
6.4. Competitive Learning   51
6.5. Data Pre-Conditioning for Competitive Learning   55
References   56

CHAPTER 7
CUSTOMIZING FOR INDUSTRIAL STRENGTH APPLICATIONS
7.1. Modeling: The Quest for Explaining and Predicting Processes   57
7.2. Combining Empiricism with Mechanistic Understanding   57
7.3. Embedding an Idealized (Partially Correct) Model   58
7.4. Embedding A Priori Understanding in the Form of Constraints   64
7.5. Incorporating Mixed Data Types   66
      7.5.1   Ordinal Digital Variables   66
      7.5.2   Nominal Digital Variables   67
7.6. Confidence Measure for Characterizing Predictions   67
7.7. Interpreting Trained Neural Net Structures   69
7.8. Graphical Interpretation of Trained Neural Net Structures   72
References   73

CHAPTER 8
CHARACTERIZING AND CLASSIFYING TEXTUAL MATERIAL
8.1. Capturing a Document's Essential Features through Fingerprinting 75
8.2. Similar Documents Auto-Classified into Distinct Clusters   76
8.3. Activity Profiles of Authors Provide Competitive Insight   77
8.4. Visualizing a Document's Contents   78
8.5. Identifying Keywords through Entropic Analysis of Text Documents 79
8.6. Automation Shrinks Time and Resources Required to Keep up
      with the World   82
References   82

CHAPTER 9
PATTERN RECOGNITION IN TIME SERIES ANALYSIS
9.1. Leading Indices as Drivers   83
9.2. Concept of Resonance in Quantifying Similarities between Time Series 83

9.3.   Identifying Leading Indicators   84
9.4.   Forecasting   86
Reference   87

CHAPTER 10
GENETIC ALGORITHMS
10.1. Background   89
10.2. Definitions   90
10.3. Setting the Stage   90
10.4. Selection   92
10.5. Mating   93
10.6. Mutation   94
10.7. "Breeding" Fit Solutions   96
10.8. Discovering Profitable Operating Strategies   98
10.9. Product Formulation   98
References   100

Part III   Case Studies

CHAPTER 11
HARNESSING THE TECHNOLOGY FOR PROFITABILITY
11.1. Process Industry Application Modes   103
       11.1.1   Plant / Unit Monitoring and Performance Prediction   103
       11.1.2   Plant Environmental Emission   104
       11.1.3   In Situ Modeling through Adaptive Learning   104
       11.1.4   Feed Translation / Property Characterization   105
       11.1.5   Product Quality Prediction   105
       11.1.6   Pilot Plant Analysis   106
       11.1.7   "Breeding" Fit Solutions   106
11.2. Business Applications   107
       11.2.1   Marketing   107
       11.2.2   Credit Risk Prediction   108
       11.2.3   Detecting Biases in Demographic Data   108
       11.2.4   Assessing Business Environments   108
       11.2.5   Competitive Intelligence   109
11.3. Case Studies that Follow   109

CHAPTER 12
REACTOR MODELING THROUGH IN SITU ADAPTIVE LEARNING
12.1.   Background   111
12.2.   Reactor Catalyst Deactivation   111
12.3.   Model Configuration   112
12.4.   In Situ Modeling Scheme   113
12.5.   Validation Procedure   115
12.6.   Validation Results   115
12.7.   Roles Played by Modeling and Plant Operational Teams   117
12.8.   Competitive Advantage Derived through this Approach   117
Reference   118

CHAPTER 13
PREDICTING PLANT STACK EMISSIONS TO MEET
ENVIRONMENTAL LIMITS
13.1.   Background   119
13.2.   Reactor Flow and Model Configuration   119
13.3.   Model Training and Results   121
13.4.   Identifying Optimal Operating Windows for Enhancing Profits   122

CHAPTER 14
PREDICTING FOULING / COKING IN FIRED HEATERS
14.1.   Background   123
14.2.   Model Configuration   123
14.3.   Model Results   125
14.4.   Conclusions   126

CHAPTER 15
PREDICTING OPERATIONAL CREDITS
15.1.   Background   127
15.2.   Issues   127
15.3.   Model Configuration   128
15.4.   Model Results   129
15.5.   Plant Follow-Up   130

CHAPTER 16
PILOT PLANT SCALE-UP BY INTERPRETING TRACER
DIAGNOSTICS
16.1.   Background   131
16.2.   Issue   131
16.3.   Genetic Algorithm–Simulation Model Coupling   132
16.4.   Results and Conclusion   135

CHAPTER 17
PREDICTING DISTILLATION TOWER TEMPERATURES: MINING
DATA FOR CAPTURING DISTINCT OPERATIONAL VARIABILITY
17.1.   Background   137
17.2.   Issue   137
17.3.   Model Configuration   137
17.4.   Identifying Distinctly Different Operating Conditions   138
17.5.   Results   139

CHAPTER 18
ENABLING NEW PROCESS DESIGN BASED ON
LABORATORY DATA
18.1.   Background   143
18.2.   Model Configuration — Bi-Level Focus for "Spot-Lighting" Region
        of Interest   143
18.3.   Model Results   145
18.4.   Conclusion   147

CHAPTER 19
FORECASTING PRICE CHANGES OF A COMPOSITE BASKET
OF COMMODITIES
19.1.   Background   149
19.2.   Approach and Model Configuration   149
19.3.   Model Results   151
19.4.   Conclusions   153

CHAPTER 20
CORPORATE DEMOGRAPHIC TREND ANALYSIS
20.1.   Background   155
20.2.   Issues   155

20.3.   Approach and Model Configuration   155
20.4.   Model Results and Conclusions   156

EPILOGUE   159

Appendices

APPENDIX A1
THERMODYNAMICS AND INFORMATION THEORY
A1.1.   Thermodynamic Concepts Set the Stage for Quantifying Information   163
A1.2.   Equilibrium as a State of Disorder — Organization as a
        Value-Adding Process   164
A1.3.   Entropy, Disorder, and Uncertainty   165
A1.4.   Opportunities Found in Imbalances   166
A1.5.   Appreciation through Quantification   167
A1.6.   Quantifying Information Transfer   167
A1.7.   Information Content in a System   168
        A1.7.1   Negentropy   169
        A1.7.2   Units of Entropy   169
        A1.7.3   Value of Information   170
References   170

APPENDIX A2
MODELING
A2.1.   What Are Models   171
A2.2.   Mechanistic Modeling — General Laws   171
A2.3.   Particular Laws and Constitutive Relations   172
A2.4.   Combining General Laws and Constitutive Relations   173
A2.5.   Modeling Directly from Data   173
Reference   173

Index   175

Part I
Philosophy

Chapter 1
Introduction

1.1. DISTINGUISHING KNOWLEDGE AND INFORMATION FROM DATA

Today we are inundated by data. This data deluge tends to overwhelm rather than be perceived for what it actually is: a significant asset for deriving competitive advantage. Realizing its value depends on the ability to extract and utilize nuggets of information and insight from these data.

Contemporary dictionaries do not make nice distinctions between *data* and *information*. We suggest thinking of *data* as quantitative or descriptive items of low intrinsic value, *information* as the enhanced result of data having been suitably organized, classified, correlated, or transformed, and *knowledge* as information processed so as to maximize its potential value by enabling effective strategies and decisions. The extraction of information from data can be viewed primitively as separating fat from meat, and the subsequent distillation of knowledge as digesting the meat. This process requires the recognition of patterns within data to uncover underlying governing phenomena as indicated in Figure 1.1, enhancing industrial operability and profitability.

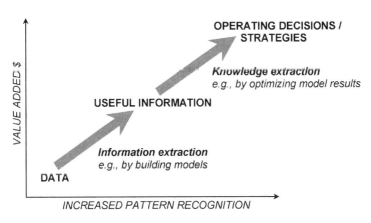

Figure 1.1. Pattern recognition adds value.

1.2. WHENCE PATTERN RECOGNITION TECHNOLOGY

The confluence of three major scientific and mathematical areas forms the foundation on which pattern recognition technology is based (Figure 1.2). These areas represent vast fields of human endeavor and achievement, in some cases spanning centuries of development, and have been and continue to be of tremendous significance and importance by themselves. That they contribute to making pattern recognition technology possible is an unintended consequence of their power, but is nonetheless a consequence of which developers and users of pattern recognition-based models and data analysis are very grateful.

The three well springs feeding pattern recognition technology are:

(1) *Thermodynamics and information theory.* Thermodynamics enables the quantification of order and its antithesis, uncertainty, through the concept of a property called entropy [1,2]. In the 1940s, Shannon [3] initiated information theory in which he drew upon thermodynamic concepts in order to quantify information.

(2) *Modeling.* Explaining and predicting the behavior of systems by building mathematical models informed by observation can be traced to the earliest

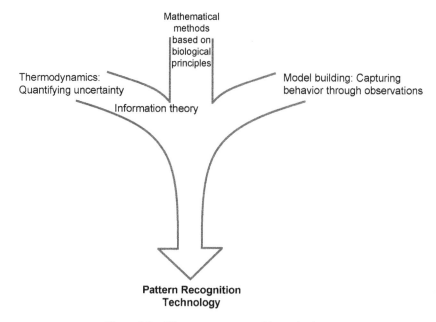

Figure 1.2.   Whence pattern recognition technology.

development of scientific method. Perhaps the model most widely known is Newton's $F = ma$ which arose from a combination of observations and subsequent deductions about forces acting on bodies.

(3) *Mathematical methods based on biological principles.* Work in this area was brought to fruition in the last two decades of the 20th century and has led to adaptive learning model building based on the ways in which we believe our brains learn. In the mid-1970s Holland [4,5] "invented" the concept of genetic algorithms, which became a very powerful optimizing methodology by incorporating the laws of evolution into a stochastic framework.

The first two of these are outlined in the rest of this chapter. They are dealt with in more detail in Appendices A1 and A2. The third one is central to the technology espoused in this book and will be explored in Chapter 3.

1.3. THERMODYNAMIC CONCEPT OF ORDER LEADING TO INFORMATION THEORY

The foundation on which thermodynamics is based makes its postulates very generally applicable. The First Law of Thermodynamics, which deals with energy conservation, can be restated in its essence as: "One cannot give that which one does not have". The implications of this should be required study for all aspiring politicians.

The Second Law of Thermodynamics deals with the direction of time's arrow, prescribing the direction in which systems will proceed naturally. This law of nature states that systems become disordered with time, and that the direction of any system's motion will be that towards a state of increasing disorder. For example, left to its own accord, a room will become progressively more "dusty". Dust will settle randomly all over the room's surfaces. The process of "dusting" a room results in increasing the order of the dust (or rather, decreasing the disorder of the dust) so that at the end of the dusting process the dust is confined to a small, designated space (i.e. a dustbin). By so confining all the dust particles to a particular location, the *uncertainty* of locating any particle of dust has been reduced to zero as we know exactly where it is. Hence, the concept of disorder (quantified by a property called entropy) is closely linked to the degree of uncertainty from an informational point of view.

Shannon [3] took advantage of this concept of uncertainty being related to a system's entropy and used the mathematical framework developed in thermodynamics to quantify information transfer. Details of this ground-laying work that came to be known as information theory are in Appendix A1.

Information theory does not address the *value* of information from a viewpoint of its usefulness; rather, it deals only with the uncertainty of outcomes expressed in the form of the number of possible options. In Appendix A1 we will break fresh and potentially controversial ground by attempting to assign value to information rather than stopping at merely quantifying the extent of uncertainty or ambiguity. We do so by invoking the thermodynamic concept of availability, which addresses the potential for doing useful work.

1.4.   MODELING INFORMED BY OBSERVATION

Models are abstractions of reality. Their purpose is to explain and predict physical, economic, or social phenomena. We relate to our environment through models. Whereas scientists and engineers use systematic mathematical formulation to build models, every human being, consciously or (most often) subconsciously, develops internalized models based on experience to yield expectations for interactions with the external world. Though models that we build are too simplified to portray reality completely, if skillfully built they can adequately explain and predict real phenomena that do not deviate too far from the domain for which they were developed. A model's merit is determined by how closely its results correspond to actual observations, and over how wide a range it is valid. It is critical that a model's user be cognizant of the domain and conditions for which a particular model yields valid results.

Gershenfeld [6] very succinctly stated that models arise from "introspection or observation (or both)". Introspection itself is informed and stimulated by observation. Our entire body of scientific understanding has been established through centuries of keen observations and ingenious connections (or correlations) derived from these observations (see Figure 1.3).

Traditionally, models have been developed by mathematically formulating phenomenological behavior after the phenomena are adequately understood. If these formulations are amenable to analytical or numerical solution, the results enable robust explanation and prediction of system behavior within the bounds of the models' regions of validity. This traditional modeling process is very costly and time-consuming, particularly for the complex phenomena from whose understanding we wish to profit.

Technical and business fronts are advancing at ever increasing rates. This accelerating pace of progress puts increasing demands on being able to assimilate

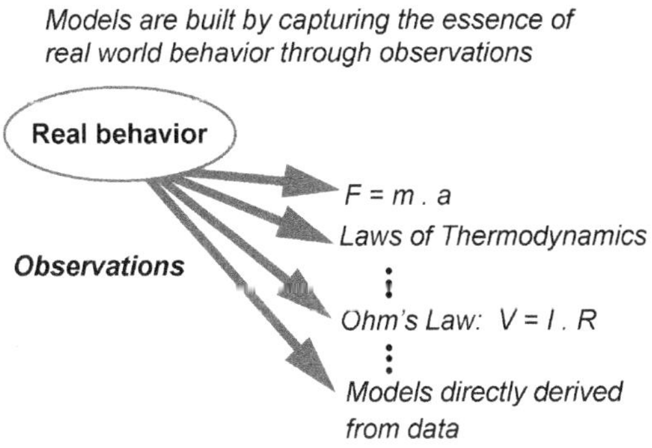

Models are built by capturing the essence of
real world behavior through observations

Real behavior

$F = m \cdot a$

Laws of Thermodynamics

Observations

$\vdots$

Ohm's Law: $V = I \cdot R$

$\vdots$

Models directly derived
from data

Figure 1.3. Relating to our environment through models.

very quickly all that is happening. Not only is the number of new processes to be modeled increasing, the levels of detail and complexity that need to be captured by predictive models in order to satisfy market forces are also increasing. Competitive advantage is gained by augmenting (or even leapfrogging) traditional modeling processes by developing robust models (automatically, if possible) directly from operating experience, i.e. data.

Developing a model for an industrial application is analogous to sonata form in classical music. Sonata form comprises of four parts: exposition; development; recapitulation; and coda; and has as its counterpoint in modeling: problem formulation (exposition); algorithm development (development); validation (recapitulation); interpretation and fruition of deployment (coda).

1.5. PATTERN RECOGNITION TECHNOLOGY TRIAD

Figure 1.4 illustrates the following technological triad on which this book is based:

(1) *Self-organizing systems.* Characterize and cluster data to quantify similarities and differences, and to identify anomalies.
(2) *Data driven adaptive learning modeling and customized neural nets.* Capture knowledge by building models directly from operating/compositional data.
(3) *Genetic algorithms.* Explore operating/composition space to discover optimal operating strategies/product formulations.

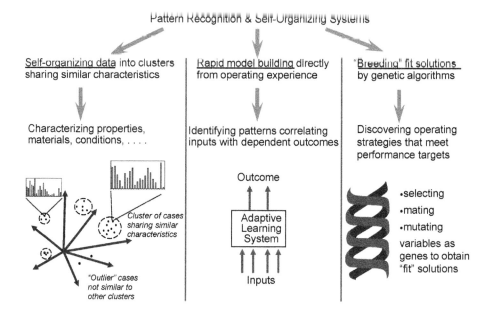

Figure 1.4.   Pattern recognition technology triad.

REFERENCES

[1] Van Wylen, G.J. & Sonntag, R.E. (1976) *Fundamentals of Classical Thermodynamics*, 2nd Edition, Wiley, New York.

[2] Schroedinger, E. (1967) *What is Life?*, Cambridge University Press, Cambridge, Reprint.

[3] Shannon, C.E. (1948) A mathematical theory of communication. *Bell Syst. Tech. J.*, **27** (3) July.

[4] Holland, J.H. (1975) *Adaptation in Natural and Artificial Systems*, The University of Michigan Press, Ann Arbor, MI.

[5] Holland, J.H. (1992) *Adaptation in Natural and Artificial Systems*, MIT Press, Cambridge, MA.

[6] Gershenfeld, N. (1999) *The Nature of Mathematical Modeling*, Cambridge University Press, Cambridge.

Chapter 2
Patterns Within Data

2.1. TYPES OF DATA

Data are expressed in various ways. We are most familiar with data expressed as numbers, e.g. stock prices, local temperature, and so on. More information is conveyed when they are expressed as sets of numbers (or vectors). Simple examples of these are the high, low, and closing stock prices for the day. Each of these three numbers is an element in a three-dimensional vector which as a whole describes the stock behavior during the day with greater texture than that contained in just the closing value. Another example of a data vector is the characterization of a crude oil sample, consisting of a set of numbers denoting the sulfur content, nitrogen content, density, and the temperatures at which 10, 50, and 90% by weight of the sample would evaporate at atmospheric pressure.

Data may also take the form of discrete or digital values such as on or off; true or false; low, medium, or high; etc. Such digital data may be binary (e.g. true or false), tertiary (e.g. low, medium, or high), or comprised of any other integral number of discrete states. These need not necessarily be amenable to ranking in a seriatim. Variables on which ranking cannot be imposed are called *nominal* variables; *ordinal* variables being those which can be placed in ranked order [1].

Much of the data we absorb every day is in the form of a natural language (such as English) through which we communicate. The study of language is an entire subject unto itself. However, a contemporary approach to modeling directly from data must entertain the idea that at times data may need to be mined from natural language text.

2.2. CHARACTERIZING DATA

The creation of order within a system (i.e. decreasing its entropy) increases the system's availability and so adds to its value. Order is synonymous with organization, the essence of which is the grouping together of similar data points and distinguishing them from dissimilar ones. The critical issues in organizing data are defining, followed by identifying and quantifying, similarities within a set of data.

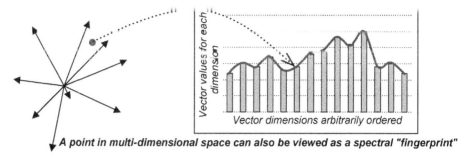

A point in multi-dimensional space can also be viewed as a spectral "fingerprint"

Figure 2.1.   Fingerprints capture conditions represented by data.

Characterizing data provides the basis on which they can be organized. If data are in the form of numbers, their numerical values or some transformation of those values often characterize them adequately. Appropriate transformation of values (also known as data pre-conditioning) is critical in enabling successful extraction of meaningful patterns. This very important process of treating data will be dealt with in greater detail later in this book.

A vector is a set of numbers, and can be represented graphically by a point in multi-dimensional space. We are accustomed to three-dimensional[1] space and most of us are unable to grasp fully a picture of higher order dimensions, as we have no physical medium in which to express such a picture. A vector in a high-dimensional space can be visualized by transforming the multi-dimensional image into a two-dimensional spectral "fingerprint" as shown in Figure 2.1, illustrating how easily a pattern can be associated with a datum point. The fingerprint curve would change its shape completely were the order of the dimensions along the *x*-axis to change. This, however, is irrelevant for pattern recognition purposes so long as the dimensional order is kept the same for all the data over the duration of the analysis.

Characterizing data becomes more complicated when data to be analyzed are comprised of combinations of different types: numbers and vectors; discrete values; text. The methodology of handling such combinations will be addressed later on. The merits of any method of characterizing data depend on how well the method facilitates identifying and quantifying similarities and differences within the data.

---

[1] Not including the dimension of time in which our motion is restricted and beyond our control.

2.3. DISTANCE BETWEEN DATA

Determining how similar or different two data points are requires the capability of measuring the distance between them. This then raises the question of defining distance in a general way.

2.3.1 Binary Data

Let us first consider the simplest kind of data: binary data consisting of strings of bits[2] (each bit having a value of 0 or 1). A well-established measure of the distance between two binary message strings, each comprised of the same number of bits, is the *Hamming distance*, defined as the sum of all the mismatches between corresponding bits in each of the messages. Two identical messages are separated by a Hamming distance of zero, whereas two messages with m mismatched bits are separated by a Hamming distance of m. Hamming [2] suggested a geometric view of binary messages to illustrate this distance. A binary message consisting of n bits can be represented as a point in n-dimensional space. If two such messages differ by a single bit, then they would inhabit adjacent vertices on the hyper-cube in this n-dimensional space, and would be separated from each other by one side of the hyper-cube. Dissimilarity between binary messages can also be expressed by normalizing the Hamming distance by the total number of bits in each message [1]. Hence, m/n and $(n - m)/n$ would be measures of the dissimilarity and similarity, respectively, between two binary messages each of length n bits and having m mismatched bits.

2.3.2 Numerical Data

One of the most common measures used for the difference between two n-dimensional vectors, $\bar{V}_i$ and $\bar{V}_j$, is the Euclidean distance (Eq. (2.1)):

$$E_{ij} = \sqrt{\sum_{k=1}^{n} (V_{ik} - V_{jk})^2} \qquad (2.1)$$

Other measures of distance have been proposed, including the city block metric [1], defined in Eq. (2.2), which is somewhat analogous to the Hamming distance

---

[2] A bit is a binary unit of measure. The word *bit* was coined by J.W. Tukey as cited in Shannon's seminal publication on information theory (Ref [5] in Appendix A1).

for binary data.

$$C_{ij} - \sum_{k=1}^{n} |V_{ik} - V_{jk}| \qquad (2.2)$$

The city block distance may be viewed as the distance between two points when one is constrained to travel peripherally around (rectangular) blocks rather than in a direct, "as the crow flies" Euclidean route.

In both these measures we can use weights, w_k, to scale variables in individual dimensions ($k = 1, ..., n$) in order to accommodate variations in the ranges of values associated with different dimensions. When weighted in this manner, the Euclidean distance becomes:

$$E_{ij} = \sqrt{\sum_{k=1}^{n} \{w_k \cdot (V_{ik} - V_{jk})^2\}} \qquad (2.3)$$

As we will see in later discussions, a far more effective and robust way of weighting dimensions is by data pre-conditioning that is customized for the particular pattern recognition or modeling method being deployed in analyzing the data.

A very effective measure of distance for purposes of pattern extraction and clustering is the angular distance between vectors. The cosine of the angle between vectors is used in determining the dot product of two vectors, as shown in Eq. (2.4).

$$D_{ij} = \frac{\sum_{k=1}^{n} (V_{ik} \cdot V_{jk})}{\sqrt{\sum_{k=1}^{n} V_{ik}^2} \cdot \sqrt{\sum_{k=1}^{n} V_{jk}^2}} \qquad (2.4)$$

We will use this measure extensively in our later treatment of auto-classifying architectures.

2.3.3   Discrete or Digital Data

It is not meaningful to associate distance for discrete data consisting of nominal variables (defined earlier) which are not amenable to ranking. Examples of such variables are colors,[3] classes of fruits or vegetables, names of vendors, etc. While it may be argued that even these types of data could be ranked by some subjective

---

[3] Colors as physical phenomena, however, result from the frequencies of emitted or reflected light, and can therefore be rank-ordered from that point of view.

measure, that would defeat the intent of our approach to feature extraction. In the case of ordinal digital data, distances may be defined using the Hamming or city block (Eq. (2.2)) methods.

2.3.4 Textual Data

Different measures of distance can be associated with textual data depending on the nature of the pattern extraction application. These measures range from being based on semantics and on qualifying or modifying descriptors, to root-word frequency maps, and will be dealt with in later chapters.

2.4. ORGANIZING DATA — CLUSTERING / AUTO-CLASSIFICATION

Data organization can be envisioned as a clustering process that identifies neighbors by their proximity to one another. Handling large amounts of data as well as dealing effectively with streams of incoming fresh data require robust self-organizing systems capable of continuously updating themselves in a dynamically adaptive manner.

Let us briefly describe an approach for auto-classifying data. The process is initiated by arbitrarily establishing clusters, and then assigning individual data to particular clusters based on the proximity of the data to the clusters' centroids.[4] Successive iterations of the data-assigning process lead to the convergence of a set of clusters capturing similar data within a pre-specified selectivity criterion. A narrow tolerance limit on the selectivity criterion results in a large number of clusters, each containing a relatively small number of very similar data; a broader tolerance yields fewer, more inclusive clusters with greater internal diversity. Cluster centroids are continually updated to adapt to their member data groups as fresh data are encountered. New clusters are created to accommodate those incoming fresh data that are too far (according to the selectivity criterion) from any existing cluster. Architectural details to construct such self-organizing systems will be dealt with in later chapters.

Organizing data in this manner enables us to identify member groups and quantify their similarities, and to predict properties of fresh incoming data by their proximity to historical data whose properties are known.

---

[4] A cluster's centroid is its center of gravity. It is a point (in the same dimensional space as the rest of the data) representing the mean of all the member data points within the cluster.

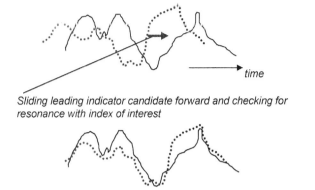

Figure 2.2.   Identifying leading indicators by checking for resonance.

2.5. ORGANIZING DATA — DATA SERIES RESONANCE

The profusion of available data today often causes an information inquiry to result in a bombardment of data streams with little indication of their relevance or importance to the original inquiry. When confronted with a number of data streams,[5] it is advantageous to determine whether or not they are interrelated and, if so, identify the interrelationships. One way of accomplishing this is by investigating the "resonance" between different data series in order to quantify the extent of their similarity and, in the case of time series, to determine the phase interval with which one series leads another (see Figure 2.2).

2.6. ORGANIZING DATA — CORRELATIVE MODELING

Extracting patterns from data so as to express cause and effect relationships is of considerable value. This entails correlating outcome to input conditions:

$$\text{outcome} = f(\text{independent input parameters}) \qquad (2.5)$$

The functional relationship f may be articulated as mathematical formulae, decision trees or logic structures, stochastic processes, computer subroutines or algorithms, analog devices, or any combination of these. In Eq. (2.5) the outcome depends on independent input parameters that govern the underlying process. Identifying these governing parameters is critical to modeling success.

---

[5] Including but not limited to time sequences.

Correlative patterns between input parameters and outcomes can be learned from experience (i.e. historical data) and then used to predict outcomes for fresh input conditions. Conventional statistical analysis has been used quite successfully for many decades to regress data. The essence of statistics deals with examining populations of data, searching for probability distribution models that characterize the populations, quantifying these distributions with suitable parameters, and ultimately discovering relationships between different variables.

Conventional statistical analysis, however, has several inherent limitations. The forms of the equations governing the phenomena being modeled need to be specified suitably. At times this may be difficult (if not impossible), especially if the underlying phenomena are not well understood, or are very complex. Poorly specified functions result in inadequate models. Furthermore, considerable mathematical and numerical difficulties need to be overcome to obtain robust convergence if the functions that need to be specified are highly non-linear.

Neural nets are mathematical constructs that identify and learn correlative patterns (should they exist) between sets of input data and corresponding outcomes from prior experience. They automatically develop non-linear internal models through an ensemble of parallel distributed basis functions. Cybenko [4] established the mathematical soundness of the foundation on which neural nets are based.[6] Neural nets obviate the need to pre-specify correlative functional forms, and alleviate any mathematical and numerical difficulties [3]. Once trained, such nets can be used to predict outcomes from fresh input data.

Neural nets were inspired by attempts to emulate the way we learn by making neural connections in our brains. Later chapters will describe their background, development, architecture, and application.

By enabling the prediction of outcomes for new conditions, empirical correlative models permit developing and testing operating strategies inexpensively and with far less risk than doing so directly in the unforgiving marketplace or manufacturing plant. Additionally, a very wide range of "what-if" scenarios can be explored to compare strategic plans under different contingencies.

REFERENCES

[1] Gordon, A.D. (1981) *Classification*, Chapman & Hall, London.
[2] Hamming, R.W. (1980) *Coding and Information Theory*, Prentice Hall, Englewood Cliffs, NJ.
[3] Bhagat, P.M. (1990) An introduction to neural nets. *Chem. Eng. Prog.*, August, 55–60.
[4] Cybenko, G. (1989) *Math. Control Signals Syst.*, **2**, 303–314.

---

[6] This is further elaborated in Chapter 3.

Chapter 3

Adapting Biological Principles for Deployment in Computational Science

Embedding biological principles into mathematical methods has yielded valuable tools for scientists and engineers. Advances in these areas include the development of adaptive learning systems patterned after biological neural networks, and very powerful optimizing algorithms resulting from incorporating genetic natural selection principles into stochastic frameworks.

3.1. LEARNING ORGANISMS — AN INTRODUCTION TO NEURAL NETS [1]

Neural nets mimic human learning processes. Humans often learn by trial and error. Consider an example of how a child learns to recognize shapes. A toy commonly given to toddlers consists of different solid shapes (triangles, squares, circles, etc.) which can be inserted into a box only through correspondingly shaped holes. The child learns about shapes by repeatedly trying to fit the solid objects through these holes. Initially, the learning cycle consists of numerous trial-and-error attempts. Eventually, however, the shapes are recognized, and the child is able to match the objects with the holes by inspection rather than by trial and error.

Neural nets operate analogously. Nets are trained iteratively on input data along with the corresponding target outcomes. After a sufficient number of training iterations, nets learn to recognize patterns (if they exist) in the data and in effect create internal models of the processes governing the data. Trained nets can be used to predict outcomes for fresh input conditions—just as the child eventually learns to recognize shapes in general.

The concepts for developing adaptive learning systems are derived from our understanding of biological neural cognitive processes. To obtain a primitive view of how biological neural systems process signals, imagine an ensemble of neurons connected to each other. A neuron is a cell which "fires," emitting an output response when it is stimulated by an input signal exceeding some threshold level. The connections[7] between neurons serve as weighting functions, ameliorating signals flowing between neurons. The strengths of these synaptic connections are

---

[7] Also known as synapses.

17

modified by adaptive experience,[n] enabling the ensemble of neurons to respond appropriately to different input stimulation.

Neural nets[9] are mathematical constructs that simulate natural adaptive learning. Two different modes of adaptive learning are particularly useful: (1) identifying and classifying distinct patterns from experienced stimuli, i.e. sorting patterns into "bins" and then recognizing which "bin" a new pattern belongs to; and (2) associating particular input patterns with corresponding outcomes. The first of these learning modes is called "unsupervised learning," as it does not require target responses to be provided for each example with which the system is trained. In contrast, "supervised learning" consists of supplying the adaptive system with suitable responses corresponding to each input pattern which it is being trained to learn.

Adaptive learning algorithms consist of the following building blocks: (i) simulated neurons; (ii) connections between neurons; and (iii) weights that modify the signals passed through these connections. Simulated neurons receive signals from other neurons, sum the signals, process the sum with a transfer function (more on which later), and then send the processed result to yet other neurons. A weight is associated with each of the connections between neurons. This weight attenuates or amplifies the signal sent to the receiving neuron. During the learning process, the weights are modified so that the net converges on learning the desired behavior. Hence, the "information content" of the net is embodied in these weights. The synaptic structure along with the weights constitutes the model internally generated by the net. It is important to note that the internal models generated by the nets do not require any specification of the forms of the equations governing the underlying phenomena being modeled. Neural nets are well suited for handling problems involving complex and highly non-linear phenomena for which adequate data are available.

It is also important to recognize the distinction between neural nets and "expert systems." The latter cannot be "taught," but have to be constructed by structuring the knowledge from human experts in an arrangement similar to a logic tree. Ensuring that expert systems encompass an adequately comprehensive range of realistic situations is an extremely arduous and cumbersome task. In contrast, neural nets learn by themselves and develop internal models of the underlying processes by absorbing field, literature, or model data directly. Though neural nets do not need any input from domain experts, embedding whatever expertise is available considerably enhances the robustness of their predictions, as we will discuss later.

---

[8] Several models have been proposed for how synaptic strengths are adapted to different learning experiences (see Refs. [2–15]).

[9] Originally called "artificial neural nets" to distinguish them from their biological predecessors.

3.2.   SUPERVISED LEARNING

Supervised learning, as suggested by its name, guides adaptive learning systems by providing appropriate responses associated with each input pattern in the training data. Iterative learning leads to converged functional correlations between independent and dependent variables. What makes these adaptive learning systems so powerful is that: (i) they can develop correlations for very complex, non-linear phenomena; (ii) they can learn from noisy data; and (iii) their empirical learning can be constrained by whatever mechanistic understanding or experience-based judgment is available to enable robust extrapolation.

A back-propagation neural net is an example of a typical adaptive learning system.

Back-propagation neural nets (Figure 3.1) are comprised of inter-connected simulated neurons. A neuron is an entity capable of receiving and sending signals and is simulated by software algorithms on a computer. As mentioned earlier, each simulated neuron (i) receives signals from other neurons, (ii) sums these signals, (iii) transforms this signal[10] and (iv) sends the result to yet other neurons. A weight, modifying the signal being communicated, is associated with each connection between neurons. The "information content" of the net is embodied in the set of all these weights that, together with the net structure, constitute the model generated by the net.

The back-propagation (or "backprop") net has information flowing in the forward direction in the prediction mode and back-propagated error corrections in the learning mode. Such nets are organized into layers of neurons. Connections are made between neurons of adjacent layers: a neuron is connected so as to receive signals from each neuron in the immediately preceding layer, and to transmit signals to each neuron in the immediately succeeding layer. A minimum of three layers is required. An input layer, as its name implies, receives input. One or more intermediate layers (also called hidden layers because they are hidden from external exposure) lie between the input layer and the output layer which communicates results externally. Additionally, a "bias" neuron supplying an invariant output is connected to each neuron in the hidden and output layers. The number of neurons used in the hidden layer depends on the number of the input and output neurons, and on the number of available training data patterns. Too few hidden neurons hinder the learning process, and too many degrade the net's generalizing capability.

An outcome from a given input condition is generated in the following way. Signals flow only in the forward direction—from input to hidden to output layers.

---

[10]The most commonly used function to transform the signal is a sigmoid, which is a monotonic, continuously differentiable, bounded function of the form $f(x) = 1/(1 + \exp(-x))$.

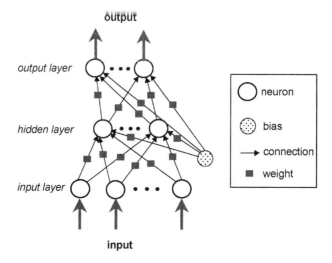

Figure 3.1. Schematic for a "backprop" neural net.

A given set of input values is imposed on the neurons in the input layer. These neurons transform the input signals and transmit the resulting values to neurons in the hidden layer. Each neuron in the hidden layer receives a signal (modified by the weight of the corresponding connection) from each neuron in the input layer. The neurons in the hidden layer individually sum up the signals they receive together with a weighted signal from the bias neuron, transform this sum and then transmit the result to each of the neurons in the next layer. Ultimately, the neurons in the output layer receive weighted signals from neurons in the pen-ultimate layer and the bias, sum the signals, and emit the transformed sums as output from the net.

The net is trained by adjusting the weights in order to minimize errors. In the learning (or training) mode, the net is supplied with sets of data comprised of values of input variables and corresponding target outcomes. The weights for each connection are initially randomized. During the training process, the errors (which are the differences between the actual output from the net and the desired target outcomes) are propagated backwards (hence the name "back-propagation") through the net and are used to update the connecting weights. Repeated iterations of this operation result in a converged set of weights and a net that has been trained to identify and learn patterns (should they exist) between sets of input data and corresponding sets of target outcomes.

Nature's propensity to produce incredibly complex organisms from very simple building blocks extends to its learning systems, and is reflected in the neural nets we build. The transforming function within each neuron is extremely simple; yet an ensemble of these functions in parallel exhibits very rich and mathematically comprehensive behavior. In an important paper establishing the mathematical soundness of the foundation on which neural nets are based, Cybenko [16] showed that "arbitrary decision functions can be arbitrarily well approximated by a neural network with one internal layer and a continuous sigmoidal non-linearity."

3.3. UNSUPERVISED LEARNING

At times we learn through instruction; at other times we learn by recognizing similarities between objects or situations, thereby making connections between different concepts, and so adding to and organizing our internal world of understanding. Neural nets designed to perform the latter type of learning do so by auto-classifying multi-dimensional data patterns. For a learning system to classify data without specifically being told how, it is essential that it be able to discover and extract characteristic features from within the data. Having done so, it can then identify and quantify similarities between previously encountered data patterns and fresh data. The following is an example of an adaptive learning system designed to classify data patterns presented to it.

Each datum point is represented by an N-dimensional vector. The self-organizing adaptive learning system has a number of input neurons, N_{in}, equal to the number of dimensions used to specify the data vectors, i.e. $N_{in} = N$. Each neuron in the next layer corresponds to a cluster, and N_{in} weights are associated with it. Hence each cluster has the same dimensionality as the vector representing each datum point. The architecture of this neural net is illustrated in Figure 3.2.

During the training process, the value of each element of a training datum vector is presented to the corresponding input neuron. The pattern presented by these N_{in} vector element values are compared to the pattern of the N_{in} weights for each cluster. The cluster whose weight pattern most closely resembles the vector's pattern "captures" that datum as one of its members provided that the similarity between these two patterns lies within a specific tolerance (or selectivity) level. If the closest

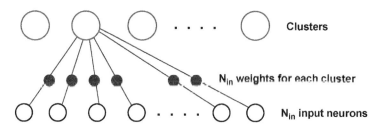

Figure 3.2. Self-organizing learning system.

pattern match is not within this tolerance, then the datum is assigned to its own separate cluster. The weights of this new cluster are set to match the datum's pattern so as to be ready to capture another datum were its pattern to be similar to this one's. On the other hand, if a datum is "captured" by a cluster already containing other data, then the weights of this cluster are adjusted slightly in order to accommodate the new datum without losing the representative pattern of the previously captured data.

Initially, all the weights are randomized. A single training iteration consists of the procedure described above in which all the training data vectors are presented one at a time to the neural net. With successive iterations the selectivity level is progressively tightened so that it asymptotically reaches a pre-specified level by the end of the training process.

As a result of undergoing this training process the data are, based on their similarities, auto-classified into clusters or groups, and outlying data that do not "fit in" with the rest are identified. If, subsequently, a fresh data pattern were to be presented to this trained net, the pattern would either be recognized as belonging to a group of other similar previously encountered patterns, or be identified as an outlier.

3.4.   MODELS THAT SELF-ORGANIZE DATA (UNSUPERVISED LEARNING) AS WELL AS CORRELATE THEM WITH DEPENDENT OUTCOMES (SUPERVISED LEARNING)

Radial Basis Function (RBF) neural nets are yet another means for self-organizing data into clusters sharing similar characteristics. This, too, is unsupervised learning in which at first only the independent parameters are presented to the model. The RBF-based methodology then attributes outcomes (or dependent

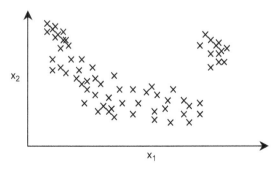

Figure 3.3.   Set of 2-D input data.

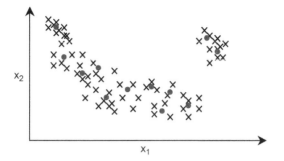

Figure 3.4. Cluster centers positioned within set of 2-D input data.

parameters) to the individual members of self-organized clusters depending on the proximity of the members to the centers of the clusters to which they belong and to other neighboring clusters.

Let us illustrate this method by considering a 2D set of input data so that it can be easily visualized. The input variables are x_1 and x_2 and hypothetical data are shown in Figure 3.3.

After specifying the number of clusters (usually an order of magnitude less than the number of available data) to characterize the data, the cluster centers are positioned within the data space in a similar manner to that employed by k-means clustering [18] as in Figure 3.4.

Depending on the data density and the proximity to other clusters, each cluster is assigned a (hyper)sphere of influence around its center [17,18] as shown in Figure 3.5. In 2D this would be a circle; in 3D a sphere; and in higher dimensional space a hypersphere.

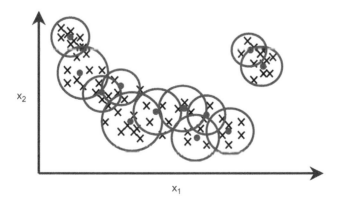

Figure 3.5. Sphere of influence assigned to each cluster.

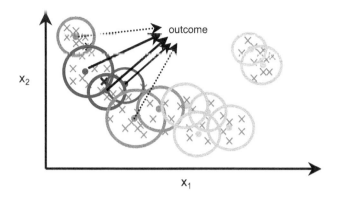

Figure 3.6. Clusters activating Gaussian functions to associate outcomes for input data.

In order to correlate independent variables with outcomes, each datum point comprised of a vector of independent variables is assigned to a particular cluster based on the proximity of the datum to the cluster's center. A Gaussian activation[11] is associated with each cluster; the Gaussian function's maximum is located at the cluster's center. Hence, a datum would activate a Gaussian signal depending on its distance from a cluster's center. The datum would activate signals from all the clusters. It would, however, elicit very weak signals from distant clusters in contrast to strong signals from nearby clusters. If each cluster were to be associated with one or more dependent outcomes, then the varying strength of the signals elicited by a particular set of independent variables would yield corresponding outcome(s) for that datum point. Figure 3.6 shows how an outcome is predicted for a point in the data space marked by the blue cross. In the figure, nearby clusters emitting strong signals are shown in red in contrast to more distant clusters responding with weaker signals.

3.5. GENETIC ALGORITHMS

Genetic algorithms incorporate natural selection principles from evolutionary biology into a stochastic framework, resulting in a very powerful optimizing methodology. Genetic algorithms are especially well suited for optimizing highly non-linear multi-dimensional phenomena which pose considerable difficulty to conventional methods particularly if the objective functions to be optimized are

---

[11]Technical details are presented in Part II (Technology).

discontinuous and/or non-monotonic. One of the main advantages of using genetic algorithms is that they are not trapped by local optima.

Genetic algorithms differ from conventional stochastic optimization techniques (such as simulated annealing) in that they are driven towards convergence by principles of natural selection. Simulated genes encode values of the independent parameters that describe the operating conditions. A set of these genes constitute a chromosome, which has an associated relative "fitness" with respect to the objective functions to be optimized depending on the values of the independent parameters (or genes). A set of independent parameters is "fitter" than another set if it yields a better (i.e. more optimal) value of the objective functions.

Genetic algorithms are initiated by randomly generating a population of chromosomes. Subsequent generations are "bred" iteratively from preceding generations through an evolutionary process consisting of favoring the selection and reproduction of fitter chromosomes, mating pairs of selected chromosomes to produce daughter chromosomes, and permitting random mutations (or changes) in the genes [19].

In selecting members for the next generation, a weighted roulette wheel is set up wherein each existing population member is assigned a segment, the size of the segment depending on the fitness of that particular member. Fitter members will have larger segments and will consequently have a greater likelihood of being represented in the next generation. It should be noted that it is not merely the fittest that are selected; with lower probability even those not so fit are given a chance for survival. Diversity turns out not only to be politically correct, but is also necessary for maximizing ultimate success in these algorithms.

This process of selecting the next generation members does not, of course, increase the members' individual fitness beyond their existing levels; the subsequent Darwinian steps to which the population is subjected accomplish that task. The members of the new generation are paired with one another stochastically; each pair becoming the parents for future daughters whose chromosomes are composed (again stochastically) of combinations of their parents' genes. Furthermore, as each gene is being transferred to the daughters, it is subject to mutation, once again on a stochastic basis.

The result at the end of several such iterations is a population containing very fit chromosomes. These chromosomes are optimized solutions to the problem. The technical details for constructing genetic algorithms are in Part II of this book.

REFERENCES

[1] Bhagat, P.M. (1990) An introduction to neural nets. *Chem. Eng. Prog.*, August.
[2] Minsky, M.L. & Papert, S.A. (1988) *Perceptrons*, expanded edition, MIT Press, Cambridge, MA.

[3] Rummelhart, D.E. & McClelland, J.L. Eds. (1986) *Parallel Distributed Processing*, vol. 1 and 2, MIT Press, Cambridge, MA.

[4] Aleksander, I. & Morton, H. (1990) *An Introduction to Neural Computing*, Chapman & Hall, London.

[5] Hebb, D.O. (1949) *The Organization of Behavior, A Neuropsychological Theory*, Wiley, New York.

[6] Stephen Judd, J. (1990) *Neural Network Design and the Complexity of Learning*, MIT Press, Cambridge, MA.

[7] Geszti, T. (1990) *Physical Models of Neural Networks*, World Scientific Publication, Singapore.

[8] Khanna, T. (1990) *Foundations of Neural Networks*, Addison-Wesley, Reading, MA.

[9] Kohonen, T. (1989) *Self-Organization and Associative Memory*, 3rd Edition, Springer, Berlin.

[10] Anderson, J.A. & Rosenfeld, E. Eds. (1988) *Neurocomputing: Foundations for Research*, MIT Press, Cambridge, MA.

[11] Anderson, J.A., Pellionisz, A. & Rosenfeld, E. Eds. (1990) *Neurocomputing 2: Directions for Research*, MIT Press, Cambridge, MA.

[12] Dayhoff, J. (1990) *Neural Network Architectures*, Van Nostrand Reinhold, New York.

[13] Wasserman, P.D. (1989) *Neural Computing*, Van Nostrand Reinhold, New York.

[14] Bishop, C.M. (1995) *Neural Networks for Pattern Recognition*, Oxford University Press, Oxford.

[15] Reed, R.D. & Marks, R.J. (1999) *Neural Smithing*, MIT Press, Cambridge, MA.

[16] Cybenko, G. (1989) *Math. Control Signals Syst.*, **2**, 303–314.

[17] Moody, J. & Darken, C.J. (1989) *Neural Comput.*, **1**, 281–294.

[18] Leonard, J.A. & Kramer, M.A. (1991) *IEEE Control Syst.*, April, 31–38.

[19] Goldberg, D.E. (1989) *Genetic Algorithms in Search, Optimization and Machine Learning*, Addison-Wesley, Reading, MA.

Chapter 4

Issues in Predictive Empirical Modeling

Robust behavior is a prerequisite for industrial-strength models. For those making operating and strategic decisions, it is imperative that the models on which their decisions are based have the following qualities. (1) They should provide adequate resolution over the range of data that span regions of operational importance. (2) They should be dependable when extrapolating. At the very least they should indicate when they are operating outside their dependable range so as to alert the user in order to adjust the level of confidence placed in them. (3) They should be accompanied by very comprehensible diagnostics and trend analyses so that the user can easily discern how they react under various conditions and in different situations. Insight into the models' behavior is critical for engendering an acceptable level of comfort in their use.

4.1. PRE-CONDITIONING DATA: PRE- AND POST-PROCESSING

An analogy can be drawn between capturing an image by means of a camera and capturing information from data by means of a model. In a camera, the field of vision is determined by the angle of its lens. A wide-angle lens will capture a broad field of vision, but with less attention to detail than will a narrow-angle lens, which focuses with greater detail on a subset of the total view. Moreover, the depth of field (i.e. the range of distance from the lens over which the image stays in focus) is inversely proportional to the diameter of the lens's aperture; as a result, more illumination is required to enable focused capture of near and distant objects simultaneously.

In the realm of modeling, the aspect of lens angle is analogous to the range used to scale the data. If, for example, the entire range over which an independent parameter could vary were used in constructing a model, then the model would encompass an overview of all possible situations with respect to that parameter. However, such a model would be less able to make fine distinctions between small variations than if a subset of the range were to have been used.

The depth of field analogy is useful in appreciating that it is easy to train a model to fit data by allowing it to have a large number of degrees of freedom. It will, however, need to be trained on a much larger set of training data in order for it to extrapolate with the same reliability as a model constrained by fewer degrees of freedom, even though the latter model may initially be more difficult to train.

Pre-conditioning data serves two purposes, both of which are essential for robust modeling. One is to focus on an appropriate data range in order to cover anticipated phenomenological activity with the desired degree of resolution. The other is to alleviate disparities in the magnitudes of values representing different variables from adversely affecting the model development by inadvertently giving more weight to certain parameters over others. Various approaches to pre- and post-processing data are described in Part II of this book. The method most appropriate for any particular application depends on the type of model being contemplated.

4.2. DETECTING EXTRAPOLATIVE CONDITIONS

Models need to be dependable under extrapolative conditions. As mentioned earlier, they should, at the very least, alert the user when the conditions, about which they are required to deliver a prediction, fall outside their domain of training. It is worth noting that in the case of non-linear models, certain conditions could be extrapolative even though the values of the independent variables for those conditions fall within the minimum and maximum values of the training data range. Harnessing the concepts discussed earlier on self-organizing data enables quantitative comparison between the input conditions, describing cases for which predictions are desired, and the original data used for developing the predictive models. It is important to flag those situations for which reliance on model predictions needs to be tempered with caution.

4.3. EMBEDDING MECHANISTIC UNDERSTANDING / EXPERIENTIAL JUDGMENT TO ENHANCE EXTRAPOLATIVE ROBUSTNESS

Not to exercise models in extrapolative modes is somewhat akin to restricting ships to dry docks. Models are most useful when they are able to predict behavior not previously encountered. We have profited immeasurably from the development and application of scientific method over many centuries. This has led to our being able to postulate what we claim to be general laws and to attain mechanistic understanding of a great many physical, chemical, and biological phenomena.

"Fundamental" models so derived enable us to extrapolate with considerable confidence in order to predict general behavior within their realm.

It follows, then, that the ideal would entail combining whatever mechanistic understanding we do have about a given process with empirical modeling methodology in order to capture the best of both worlds, viz., very rapid data-driven model development and robust extrapolative capability. That is indeed accomplished by hybrid models that embed mechanistic understanding, or experience-based judgment, into neural net models which are trained on historical data. In effect, these hybrids "triangulate" from the nearest dependable data point, extending behavioral prediction based on a combination of empiricism and fundamental understanding. The greatest advantage is obtained by enabling flexibility between building in empiricism and embedding mechanistic understanding, depending on the extent of knowledge available regarding the given phenomenon, and the range of and degree of confidence in the data.

4.4. INSIGHT INTO MODEL BEHAVIOR

A major challenge that needs to be addressed in successfully delivering neural net and other pattern recognition-based models to technically literate clients, is alleviating their concern about being given a "black box". Understandably, scientists and engineers have a great deal of comfort with facilely articulated equations because that is what they have been "brought up" on. They like to feel that they have a fundamental understanding of how the independent parameters affect the dependent outcomes.

Engineers, for example, are very comfortable with describing turbulent heat transfer using non-dimensional equations of the form shown in Eq. (4.1):

$$Nu \approx Re^n Pr^m \qquad (4.1)$$

where Nu, Re, and Pr are non-dimensional parameters, and n and m are fractional exponents.

While Re and Pr have real physical significance,[12] when raised to fractional powers they have no discernible physical meaning; the exponents are obtained through an empirical curve-fit. However, Eq. (4.1) is a staple in a thermal scientist's educational diet and has thereby been internalized, engendering scientific confidence and comfort.

---

[12]Re is the Reynolds number that characterizes fluid flow by the ratio of viscous to non-viscous forces acting on the fluid. Pr is the Prandtl number expressing the relative extent to which convection or conduction dominates in transferring heat within a fluid.

It becomes incumbent upon pattern recognition-based modelers to enable users of their models to gain insight into the models' behavior, consequently providing an acceptable degree of comfort and confidence. The most effective means of accomplishing this are:

(1) dissecting and representing a model's structure in a meaningful way;
(2) visualizing a model's performance under dynamically changing conditions.

Technical details for both of these will be addressed in Part II.

Part II
Technology

Chapter 5
Supervised Learning — Correlative Neural Nets

5.1. SUPERVISED LEARNING WITH BACK-PROPAGATION NEURAL NETS

Back-propagation[13] (BP) neural nets as automatic correlative model-builders were qualitatively described in Chapter 3. That chapter discussed their architecture, the components forming the building blocks from which they are constructed, and how they work. These nets derive their name from the training process during which the weights, modifying the strength of the connections between their neurons, are adjusted by back propagating errors through the net structure. The BP learning process enables the nets to capture essential correlative relationships between independent variables governing the phenomena and the dependent outcomes, directly from operating data.

5.2. FEEDFORWARD — EXERCISING THE BP NET IN PREDICTIVE MODE — NEURON TRANSFORMATION FUNCTION

In a seeming contradiction of terms, BP nets are members of a family of "feedforward" neural nets. Information flows in only one (forward) direction[14] when the nets are in the predictive mode; whereas errors are propagated backwards while the nets are being trained.

The BP neural net is trained on sets of data comprising of input and corresponding target values. The input data is an $n \times p$ matrix where n is the number of input variables and p the number of different training data patterns. A set of m target output variables, corresponding to m output neurons in the net, is associated with each of the p patterns. The object of the training exercise is to enable the net to identify and learn correlative relations between the n input variables and the corresponding m outputs from all the data patterns. In the predictive mode, the net is presented a set of n input variables and is required to predict m outcome variables for that set of inputs.

---

[13]Such nets are also known as "backprop" nets.

[14]from neurons in preceding layers to those in succeeding layers; i.e. information proceeds from neurons in the input layer to neurons in the hidden layer, and henceforward to neurons in the output layer.

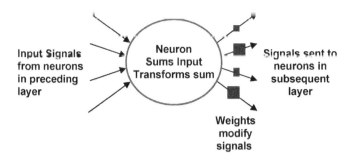

Figure 5.1. Feedforward information flow through a neuron.

The input data are directly fed as signals to the input neurons. These signals then undergo a non-linear transformation and are sent to neurons in the next layer through weighted connections. Each input layer neuron sends a (differently) weighted signal to every neuron in the next layer. Each neuron in the next layer sums up all the signals received from the preceding layer, transforms the sum, and sends the transformed sum through yet another set of weighted connections to every neuron in the subsequent layer (Figures 5.1 and 5.2).

The choice of the *transformation function* within each neuron is critical to the net's performance. Biological neurons are believed to incorporate step functions: they "fire" if their input signals exceed some threshold level. Early artificial neural nets used this approach. However, because of the overly simplistic nature of step functions, an inordinately large number of neurons so equipped were needed to

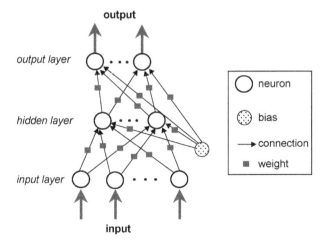

Figure 5.2. Structure of BP net.

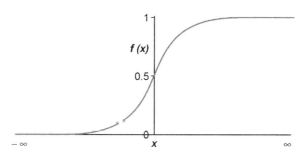

Figure 5.3. Sigmoid function.

represent arbitrarily complex behavior. Performance was vastly improved by using sigmoidal functions (shown in Eqs. (5.1) and Figure 5.3) within BP neurons. While an individual sigmoid may not be particularly interesting or powerful in modeling a complex phenomenon, an ensemble of such functions in parallel exhibits extremely rich mathematical behavior [1].

$$f(x) = \frac{1}{1 + \exp(-x)} \qquad (5.1)$$

The sigmoid function has three important properties that make it ideal for application in BP nets: it is bounded,[15] monotonic, and continuously differentiable. It is also worth noting that there is a region of sensitivity within which the function is very responsive to changes in the incoming signal, and outside of which it is relatively insensitive to the input. A later section will account for this characteristic when developing methodology for pre-conditioning data for BP nets.

A sigmoid in BP nets transforms an input into an output signal for each neuron *i* as indicated by Eq. (5.2)

$$O_{i,p} = f(I_{i,p}) = \frac{1}{1 + \exp(-I_{i,p})} \qquad (5.2)$$

where $I_{i,p}$ is the input to neuron *i* for a training datum pattern *p*, and $O_{i,p}$ is the output from neuron *i*.

The input to neuron *j* in a hidden or output layer is:

$$I_{j,p} = \sum_{i} (w_{ij} \cdot O_{i,p}) + w_{Bj} O_B \qquad (5.3)$$

---

[15]It also sometimes called a "squashing function" as it "squashes" an input ranging from $-\infty$ to $+\infty$ to an output between 0 and 1.

The sum over i represents the input received from all the neurons in the preceding layer and B represents the bias neuron. The weights w_{ij} are associated with the connections from neuron i to neuron j,[16] and w_{Bj} represents the weight of the connection from the bias neuron to neuron j. The output from the bias neuron, O_B, is invariant.

The output from a neuron in either a hidden or the output layer is obtained by substituting the input value obtained from Eq. (5.3) into the exponent in Eq. (5.2). Thus the output signals from neurons in each layer are summed to form the input signals to neurons in subsequent layers after being modified by appropriate connection weights.

5.3. BP TRAINING — CONNECTION WEIGHTS ADJUSTED BY THE "DELTA RULE" TO MINIMIZE LEARNING ERRORS

Model errors are discrepancies between calculated outputs and specified intended target values. These errors may be quantified by means of a variety of functional forms. The form most commonly used is the sum of squared errors (Eq. (5.4)). The factor of 2 in the denominator provides algebraic convenience for subsequent operations

$$\text{Error} = E = \frac{1}{2} \sum_p \sum_k (T_{k,p} - O_{k,p})^2 \tag{5.4}$$

where $T_{k,p}$ is the target value for data pattern p and output variable k.

The goal of back-propagation is to adjust all the weights in the net so as to minimize E. This is accomplished by applying the gradient descent methodology, which is:

$$\Delta w \approx -\nabla_w E \tag{5.5}$$

The training process is initiated with a randomized set of weights. Subsequent iterations update the weights in the direction of the steepest descent using an adjustable learning rate, η, in the "delta rule":

$$\Delta w = -\eta \cdot \nabla_w E \tag{5.6}$$

An infinitesimally small learning rate, required for realizing true steepest descent, would lead to extremely inefficient convergence. Larger values of η would speed

---

[16]In the literature, the nomenclature for weight subscripts is occasionally reversed from that used here. In this text we use w_{ij} to represent the weight in the connection from neuron i to neuron j; the reader may find w_{ij} used elsewhere in the literature to represent the very same connection.

up the learning process with, however, the deleterious side effect of introducing oscillations caused by over-shooting. Adding a momentum term in which the weight changes from the previous iteration provide an inertial effect through a momentum factor, α, ameliorates the side effect of oscillations

$$\Delta_t w = -\eta \cdot \nabla_w E + \alpha \cdot \Delta_{t-1} w \tag{5.7}$$

where t is the iteration counter.

5.4. BACK-PROPAGATION EQUATIONS FOR GENERAL TRANSFORMATION FUNCTIONS [2,4]

Let us now derive back-propagation weight adjustment equations for a general neuron transformation function $f(x)$. The error due to the difference between the actual output from the net and the target for the output layer neuron k for a single data pattern p is:

$$E_{k,p} = \frac{1}{2}(T_{k,p} - O_{k,p})^2 \tag{5.8}$$

The error gradient with respect to the weights is:

$$-\frac{\partial E_{k,p}}{\partial w_{jk}} = -\frac{\partial E_{k,p}}{\partial I_{k,p}} \cdot \frac{\partial I_{k,p}}{\partial w_{jk}} = -\frac{\partial E_{k,p}}{\partial O_{k,p}} \cdot \frac{\partial O_{k,p}}{\partial I_{k,p}} \cdot \frac{\partial I_{k,p}}{\partial w_{jk}} \tag{5.9}$$

where $I_{k,p}$ is the summed input to neuron k.
  Differentiating Eq. (5.8) yields:

$$\frac{\partial E_{k,p}}{\partial O_{k,p}} = -(T_{k,p} - O_{k,p}) \tag{5.10}$$

The output from a neuron is the transformed function of the summed input $I_{k,p}$ to the neuron:

$$O_{k,p} = f(I_{k,p}) \tag{5.11}$$

Therefore,

$$\frac{\partial O_{k,p}}{\partial I_{k,p}} = f'(I_{k,p}) \tag{5.12}$$

The summed input to neuron k from all j neurons (including the bias) in the preceding layer is:

$$I_{k,p} = \sum_j (w_{jk} \cdot U_{j,p}) \tag{5.13}$$

Therefore, the derivative of the summed input to k with respect to the weight connecting it to a specific neuron j in the preceding layer is:

$$\frac{\partial I_{k,p}}{\partial w_{jk}} = \frac{\partial}{\partial w_{jk}} (w_{jk} \cdot O_{j,p}) = O_{j,p} \tag{5.14}$$

The error signal generated by output neuron k for data pattern p is defined as:

$$\delta_{k,p} \equiv -\frac{\partial E_{k,p}}{\partial I_{k,p}} = (T_{k,p} - O_{k,p}) \cdot f'(I_{k,p}) \tag{5.15}$$

Therefore,

$$-\frac{\partial E_{k,p}}{\partial w_{jk}} = \delta_{k,p} \cdot O_{j,p} \tag{5.16}$$

Hence, the connection weights leading to the output neuron can be adjusted thus

$$\underset{t}{\Delta} w_{jk} = \eta \cdot \delta_{k,p} \cdot O_{j,p} + \alpha \cdot \underset{t-1}{\Delta} w_{jk} \tag{5.17}$$

here j denotes neurons in the preceding (hidden) layer.

Let us now develop equations for back-propagating the error to adjust the connection weights for the hidden neurons. The error signals $\delta_{k,p}$ from the output neurons k are propagated backwards using the chain rule to yield error signals for the j neurons in the hidden layer:

$$\delta_{j,p} = -\sum_k \frac{\partial E_{k,p}}{\partial I_{j,p}} = -\sum_k \frac{\partial E_{k,p}}{\partial I_{k,p}} \frac{\partial I_{k,p}}{\partial I_{j,p}} = \sum_k \delta_{k,p} \frac{\partial \{w_{jk} \cdot f(I_{j,p})\}}{\partial I_{j,p}}$$

$$= \sum_k \left\{ \delta_{k,p} \cdot \left(f(I_{j,p}) \cdot \frac{\partial w_{jk}}{\partial I_{j,p}} + w_{jk} \cdot f'(I_{j,p}) \right) \right\} \tag{5.18}$$

However, the uni-directional nature of back-propagation requires w_{jk} to be independent of the input to j.

Therefore,

$$\delta_{j,p} = f'(I_{j,p}) \cdot \sum_k (\delta_{k,p} \cdot w_{jk}) \tag{5.19}$$

The connection weights w_{ij} between input layer neurons i and hidden neurons j can then be adjusted using:

$$\underset{t}{\Delta} w_{ij} = \eta \cdot \delta_{j,p} \cdot O_{l,p} + \alpha \cdot \underset{t-1}{\Delta} w_{ij} \tag{5.20}$$

5.5. BACK-PROPAGATION EQUATIONS FOR SIGMOIDAL TRANSFORMATION FUNCTIONS

Sigmoidal transformation functions (Eq. (5.1)) are most commonly used in BP nets. In this section, we first need to derive an expression for the differential of Eq. (5.1) to use in Eqs. (5.15) and (5.19). From Eq. (5.1) we obtain

$$\exp(-x) = \frac{1}{f(x)} - 1 \tag{5.21}$$

and

$$f^2(x) = \frac{1}{\{1 + \exp(-x)\}^2} \tag{5.22}$$

Differentiating Eq. (5.1):

$$f'(x) = \frac{\exp(-x)}{\{1 + \exp(-x)\}^2} \tag{5.23}$$

Substituting Eqs. (5.21) and (5.22) in Eq. (5.23), we obtain

$$f'(x) = f(x) \cdot \{1 - f(x)\} \tag{5.24}$$

where $f(x)$ is the sigmoid

$$f(x) = \frac{1}{1 + \exp(-x)}$$

Using Eq. (5.24) in Eqs. (5.15) and (5.19) to obtain the error signals, δ, enables us to determine the weight adjustments (Eqs. (5.17) and (5.20)) and completes the back-propagation formulation. Recognizing that $f(I) = O$, Eqs. (5.15) and (5.19) in conjunction with Eq. (5.24) become

$$\delta_{k,p} = (T_{k,p} - O_{k,p}) \cdot O_{k,p} \cdot (1 - O_{k,p}) \tag{5.25}$$

and

$$\delta_{j,p} = O_{j,p}\cdot(1 - O_{j,p})\cdot \sum_{k} (\delta_{k,p}\cdot w_{jk})$$
(5.26)

5.6. CONJUGATE GRADIENT METHODOLOGY FOR RAPID AND ROBUST CONVERGENCE [3–5]

The basic back-propagation method prescribes adjusting the net's weights for each training datum pattern taken one at a time. This is inefficient from the point of view of rapid and robust convergence. A far better approach is to use all the data simultaneously and employ the conjugate gradient method in establishing the direction of weight convergence.

The direction of descent is determined by the sum of the individual descent vectors for the training data. This overall descent direction is calculated separately for each datum before any weight change is implemented. The steepest descent direction for changing the weight w_{ij} towards error minimization convergence for each training pattern p is

$$m_{ij,p} = \delta_{j,p}\cdot O_{i,p}$$
(5.27)

where the error signals, δ, are determined from Eqs. (5.25) or (5.26) depending on whether or not the neurons are in the output layer. The overall descent direction is the vector obtained by summing Eq. (5.27) for all the connection weights over all the training data p:

$$\bar{M} = \sum_{p} \bar{m}_p$$
(5.28)

The conjugate gradient method [3] yields the search direction for the weight adjustment

$$\underset{t}{\Delta \bar{w}} = \bar{M} + \alpha\cdot \underset{t-1}{\Delta \bar{w}}$$
(5.29)

in which the momentum factor,[17] α, is calculated as

$$\alpha = \frac{\|\bar{M}_t\|^2}{\|\bar{M}_{t-1}\|^2}$$
(5.30)

where t is the iteration counter.

---

[17]At the start of the algorithm the initial value of $\alpha = 0$.

It should be noted that Eq. (5.29) is the search direction for the weight adjustment, not the weight adjustment itself, which is then obtained by using the learning rate, thus:

$$\underset{t}{\Delta} w_{ij} = \eta \cdot \underset{t}{\Delta} \bar{w}_{ij} \tag{5.31}$$

The learning rate, η, determines the step size for the weight adjustment. The value of η is initially very small[18] and is then increased[19] for subsequent steps in the same search direction until the line search fails (i.e. the error starts to increase), at which point the last adjustment is retracted and the learning rate is reduced by a factor.[20] This retraction exercise is repeated until either the error starts to decrease, or the line search fails a pre-specified number of times.[21] If the error decreases on reducing the learning rate, then the descent direction is recalculated (Eq. (5.29)), η is reset to its initial value, and further weight adjustments to reduce the error are resumed. The retraction test fails if the error does not decrease after reducing the learning rate the pre-specified number of times. In that case, the entire procedure is restarted by determining a fresh search direction (Eq. (5.28)), and resetting η to its initial value and the momentum factor to zero. In any event, the momentum factor is reset to zero periodically when the number of iterations[22] since the last reset equals the number of connection weights plus one [3].

It is customary to stop training when the error does not decrease on resetting the search direction. For industrial applications, however, it is advisable to store the set of weights associated with the smallest error and then to continue the training process, "uphill" if necessary, in order to explore the existence of other regions of potential value.

5.7. SEPARATING SIGNAL FROM NOISE IN TRAINING

It is important not to "over-fit" the data. The standard practice of cross-validation (also sometimes called "jack-knifing") can be employed[23] to guard against doing so. This approach, however, requires the building and testing of multiple models. In cases where adequate data[24] are available, a reasonably robust preliminary

---

[18]An initial value of 0.025 is suggested.

[19]By 50% for each step.

[20]The suggested reduction factor is 0.8.

[21]10 times is suggested for this retraction exercise.

[22]An iteration being demarcated by the resetting of the search direction using equation (5.28)

[23]This method is detailed in a later chapter.

[24]Adequacy of data refers to both quantity and quality. By quality we mean how well the range of independent parameters are represented within the data set. Clustering technology (detailed in a later chapter) is useful in determining the extent of this representation, and whether it covers anticipated conditions where the model may be required to make predictions.

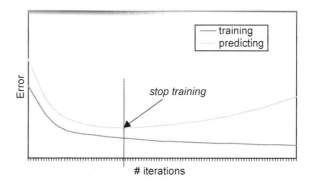

Figure 5.4. Preventing "over-fitting".

model may very quickly be obtained by setting aside a randomly selected small subset of the data as a validation sample, and training the neural net on the remaining data as outlined below.

After each iteration (demarcated by the resetting of the search direction), the errors from both the training and prediction data sets need to be recorded. The training should be stopped when the predictive error (rather than the training error) is minimized as illustrated in Figure 5.4.

In actual practice, as the error curves are rarely as smooth as those shown in this figure, judgment needs to be exercised in choosing the appropriate stopping point. It is clear that in order to recover retroactively the set of training weights at this stopping point, the training process has to be restarted and the model retrained over the optimal number of iterations. This can be accomplished reliably by using the same seed and random number-generating algorithm[25] in initializing the net the second time around.

5.8. PRE-CONDITIONING DATA FOR BP NETS

We discussed reasons for pre-conditioning data in Chapter 4. These include focusing on an appropriate data range in order to cover anticipated phenomenological activity with the desired degree of resolution. Another reason is the need to prevent disparities in the magnitudes of values, representing different variables, from adversely affecting the model development by inadvertently giving more weight to certain parameters over others. In addition

---

[25]While there are many random number-generating algorithms in the literature to choose from, a very simple one giving acceptable results for random numbers between 0 and 1 is to use the fractional part of $(\pi + \text{seed})^5$ where the seed is the previously generated random number.

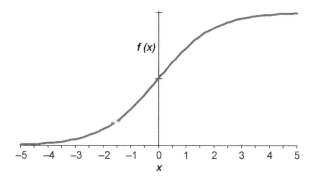

Figure 5.5. Sigmoid function—range and sensitivity.

to these general issues we need to take into account the selective sensitivity of the sigmoidal function.

Figure 5.5 shows that the function is sensitive in the range $x \cong \pm 2.5$. Hence, if the signals were scaled to lie within ± 1.75, not only would the sensitivity criterion be satisfied, but there would also be sufficient "head-room" for potential excursions in fresh data which the model may need to accommodate in the future.

Each variable is scaled by zero centering the pre-processed transformed variable using the mean for that variable over all the data patterns. Further, the variables need to be pre-processed such that either (i) all the scaled data lie within the ± 1.75 sensitive band, or (ii) a suitable range is chosen for bounding the data at the 2σ level.

The input variables may be pre-processed using Eq. (5.32a). As the input layer neurons will use sigmoids to transform input signals presented to the net for training or for prediction, the input variables should be scaled to lie between -1.75 and $+1.75$.

$$I_{\text{Scaled}}(i,p) = \{(I(i,p) - \text{Mean}(i))\cdot \text{Limit}\cdot 2\}/\{\text{Max}(i) - \text{Min}(i)\} \quad (5.32a)$$

where $I(i,p)$ is the value of the input variable i in data set p; Mean(i), Max(i) and Min(i) are the mean, maximum and minimum, respectively, of variable i over all the data set patterns; and Limit $= 1.75$.

The net emits output signals of values between 0 and 1, having processed them with sigmoidal functions in the output layer neurons. Therefore, pre-processing output variables require them to be scaled such that their pre-transformed values lie between -1.75 and $+1.75$. Eq. (5.32b) scales output variables to conform to this criterion.

$$O_{\text{Scaled}}(j,p) = \cfrac{1}{1 + \cup^{\{-(O(j,p)-\text{Mean}(j))\cdot\text{Limit}\cdot 2/(\text{Max}(j)-\text{Min}(j))\}}} \quad (5.32b)$$

where $O(j,p)$ is the value of the output variable j in data set p; Mean(j), Max(j) and Min(j) are the mean, maximum and minimum, respectively, of variable j over all the data set patterns; and Limit $= 1.75$.

Post-processing the output from the net requires the inverse operation of Eq. (5.32b) in order that the scaled output is reconverted to its original form. Equation (5.33) performs this operation:

$$O(j,p) = \frac{-(\mathrm{Max}(j) - \mathrm{Min}(j))}{\mathrm{Limit}\cdot 2} \cdot \log_e\left\{\frac{1}{O_{\mathrm{Scaled}}(j,p)} - 1\right\} + \mathrm{Mean}(j) \quad (5.33)$$

Similarly, other expressions can be developed were it desirable to scale the variable ranges by the standard deviations rather than by imposing fixed minimum and maximum limits. A later chapter will discuss pre-conditioning data from point of view of focusing attention on specific regions within the data space should finer resolution be called for to meet special needs for a particular phenomenon or process being modeled.

5.9. SUPERVISED LEARNING WITH RADIAL BASIS FUNCTION NEURAL NETS

Radial basis functions (RBF) enable a powerful technique for self-organizing multi-dimensional data. The concepts behind this auto-clustering methodology were described in Chapter 3. Its use in organizing data puts it in the class of unsupervised learning, and that aspect of its application will be dealt with in a later chapter. A supervised learning addendum can be attached to the end of its clustering capability, enabling it to become a correlative model-building tool [6,7].

Section 3.4 qualitatively described the RBF methodology: positioning cluster centers within multi-dimensional data; assigning (hyper)spheres of influence to each cluster; activating Gaussian functions associated with the clusters depending on the proximity of the cluster centers from the activating point in the data space; and associating outcomes to the Gaussian activation. The next sections contain technical details to accomplish this.

5.10. SEEDING THE INPUT DATA SPACE WITH RBF CLUSTER CENTERS

The cluster centers have the same number of dimensions as the data. The number of clusters[26] used to characterize the data needs to be specified. The process of distributing the clusters within the data space is started by initially assigning the

---

[26]10% of the training data points is a good starting point for this number. As we will see in later chapters, the finalized model for industrial deployment should follow a validating exercise in which several candidate models with varying numbers of clusters are tested.

cluster centers to coincide with randomly selected data points. The following procedure is then iterated until convergence is reached in positioning the cluster centers.

The Cartesian distance between each cluster center and each datum point is determined.

$$D_{pj} = \sqrt{\sum_i (I_{i,p} - C_{i,j})^2} \tag{5.34}$$

where j is the cluster number, p the data pattern, $I_{i,p}$ is value of the input variable from data pattern p in the i dimension, and $C_{i,j}$ is the i dimensional position of cluster j.

The closest cluster to each training data point is then identified, and that cluster is assigned to that datum.

$$\text{Closest}(p) = j_{\text{closest}} \tag{5.35}$$

where j_{closest} is the closest cluster to datum p.

The cluster centers are then moved to the centroid of the data associated with them. This is done by calculating the centroid of the data "captured" by each cluster, moving the cluster center to that position, and noting the displacement from the previous position.[27] The new position of the cluster center is

$$C_{i,j} = \frac{\sum_{p'} I_{i,p'}}{N_{p'}} \tag{5.36}$$

where $C_{i,j}$ is the i dimensional position of cluster center j, p' are the data captured by cluster j, and $N_{p'}$ are the number of those captured data.

The movement of the cluster center after iteration t is:

$$\Delta C_{i,j} = C_{i,j}|_t - C_{i,j}|_{t-1} \tag{5.37}$$

This process is repeated: the distance between the newly positioned cluster centers and all the data are calculated; the cluster membership is reassigned based on the proximity of data to cluster centers; and the cluster centers are repositioned at the centroid of the current data membership. The iterations are terminated when the cluster centers have equilibrated. This is deemed to occur when $\Delta C_{i,j}$ for all j clusters and i dimensions is less than a pre-specified tolerance level.

---

[27]Convergence of this unsupervised training is established when the centers cease to move further.

5.11. ASSIGNING SPHERES OF INFLUENCE TO EACH CLUSTER

As mentioned earlier, each cluster exerts a sphere of influence in the data space. This constitutes a circle in 2D, a sphere in 3D, and a hyper-sphere in higher order dimensions. In this section, the radius of this (hyper) sphere will be determined for each cluster based on the nearest two-neighbor k-means clustering convention.

The Cartesian distances between cluster centers is first calculated

$$\text{RBFdist}(j_1, j_2) = \sqrt{\sum_i (C_{i,j_1} - C_{i,j_2})^2} \qquad (5.38)$$

where $\text{RBFdist}(j_1, j_2)$ is the distance between the centers of clusters j_1 and j_2.

Next, the two nearest neighbors of each cluster are identified. Let j_2 and j_3 be the nearest and the second-nearest neighbors, respectively, of cluster j_1. The radius of the sphere of influence exerted by cluster j_1 is then given by:

$$r_{j_1} = \sqrt{\frac{\text{RBFdist}(j_1, j_2)^2 + \text{RBFdist}(j_1, j_3)^2}{2}} \qquad (5.39)$$

5.12. ACTIVATING CLUSTERS FROM A POINT IN THE DATA SPACE

Each cluster exerts a Gaussian influence on the space around it. The Gaussian signal is at its maximum value at the cluster's center, and drops of inversely as the square of the distance from the center. Hence, the activation, A_{cp}, of any point p in the data space due to cluster c is

$$A_{cp} = \exp(-[D_{pc}]^2/[r_c]^2) \qquad (5.40)$$

where D_{pc} is the distance between data point p and the center of cluster c; and r_c is the radius of the hyper-sphere of influence of cluster c.

During the training process, after the cluster centers and radii have been assigned, weights ($w_{c,k}$) are determined (detailed in Section 3.11) linking each cluster c with the dependent outcome variable k based on target outcomes prescribed by the training data set. An additional, common (to all clusters) bias weight, $w_{\text{Bias},k}$, is determined by linear regression for each dependent outcome variable k. The non-linearity inherent in the phenomena is modeled by the Gaussian functions characterizing the independent variable space. These Gaussian functions are then linearly mapped to yield dependent outcomes. The outcome for any point d in the data space is predicted by determining the extent of activation by d of all N clusters in conjunction with the weights linking each cluster with the corresponding output variable

$$\text{Outcome}_{p,k} = \sum_{c=1}^{N} \{A_{cp} \cdot w_{c,k}\} + w_{\text{Bias},k} \tag{5.41}$$

where N is the total number of clusters in the model, k is the output variable, and $w_{c,k}$ is the weight connecting cluster c with output variable node k.

5.13. DEVELOPING RBF CORRELATION MODELS — ASSIGNING WEIGHTS TO MAP OUTCOME [7]

As mentioned earlier, any phenomenological non-linearity is captured by the Gaussian functions. The remaining step in creating a correlative model is to assign a weight between each cluster's activation and each outcome variable. This is done by determining a set of weights, $w_{c,k}$, that minimizes $\|\mathbf{T} - \mathbf{wA}\|^2$, where $\mathbf{T}$ is the $K \times P$ matrix of target outcomes for all K variables and P data patterns, $\mathbf{w}$ is the $K \times N$ matrix of weights for all N clusters, and $\mathbf{A}$ is the $N \times P$ activation matrix resulting from the training data input exciting the cluster centers.

The weights are determined by linearly solving Eq. (5.42):

$$\mathbf{w} = \mathbf{TA}^{\mathbf{T}}(\mathbf{AA}^{\mathbf{T}})^{-1} \tag{5.42}$$

5.14. PRE-CONDITIONING DATA FOR RBF NETS

The output variables do not need pre-conditioning in RBF nets because the activation functions are mapped linearly to give a least squares fit to the target values. Barring any special needs for focusing on certain regions of the input space, a very simple yet robust pre-processing approach is to compress each input variable linearly into an interval between 0 and 1.

5.15. NEURAL NET CORRELATION MODELS

The neural net structures described in this chapter constitute the basic "workhorses" for the rapid development of correlative models. Later chapters will deal with special refinements and modifications that will enhance their capabilities, making them very suitable candidates for building adaptive, industrial-strength models that learn directly from operating and historical data.

REFERENCES

[1] Cybenko, G. (1989) *Math. Control Signals Syst.*, **2**, 303–314.
[2] Rummelhart, D.E. & McClelland, J.L. Eds. (1986) Parallel Distributed Processing, vol. 8, MIT Press, Cambridge, MA, Chapter 8.
[3] Leonard, J. & Kramer, M.A. (1990) *Comput. Chem. Eng.*, **14** (3), 337–341.
[4] Bishop, C.M. (1995) *Neural Networks for Pattern Recognition*, Oxford University Press, Oxford.
[5] Reed, R.D. & Marks, R.J. (1999) *Neural Smithing*, MIT Press, Oxford.
[6] Moody, J. & Darken, C.J. (1989) *Neural Comput.*, **1**, 281–294.
[7] Leonard, J.A. & Kramer, M.A. (1991) *IEEE Control Syst.*, April, 31–38.

Chapter 6
Unsupervised Learning: Auto-Clustering and Self-Organizing Data

6.1. UNSUPERVISED LEARNING — VALUE TO INDUSTRY

Contemporary businesses acquire and store mind-boggling amounts of data describing their operations and transactions. These potential treasure troves of information remain largely untapped on account of their overwhelming volume, and rather than being used profitably to guide decision making, they burden the organizations' resources. The need for unsupervised learning systems that can self-organize these data meaningfully is self-evident.

Unsupervised learning involves the discovery and extraction of characteristic features from a large number of cases and the subsequent organization of these cases into groups sharing similar attributes without any superimposed prescription or guidance. The literature is replete with numerous unsupervised learning algorithms ranging from an exposition of fundamental concepts in Ref. [1] and Kohonen's self-organizing maps [2,3], to Grossberg's adaptive resonance (ART) [4,5], and many others. In this book, we will focus on two powerful approaches that have been proven very effective in industrial applications. The first one, Radial Basis Functions (RBF) methodology detailed in Chapter 5, constitutes one of the ways in which multi-dimensional data can be self-organized. Competitive learning is the other approach, as described qualitatively in Section 3.3, in which data are self-organized by clusters competing for member data based on their proximity to each other. Our implementation of competitive learning combines various features from different approaches in order to make for an effective industrial tool. Sections 6.2 and 6.3 will recapitulate the quantitative aspects of RBF as applied to auto clustering, and competitive learning will be elucidated mathematically in Section 6.4.

6.2. AUTO-CLUSTERING USING RADIAL BASIS FUNCTIONS

The mathematical details related to RBF were presented in Chapter 5. The salient expressions for deploying this methodology in unsupervised learning are reiterated here.

The data space is seeded with RBF cluster centers. This process is initiated by assigning the cluster centers to coincide with randomly selected data points. The distance between each cluster center and each datum point is then determined as in Eq. (6.1)

$$D_{pj} = \sqrt{\sum_i (I_{i,p} - C_{i,j})^2}$$ (6.1)

where j is the cluster number, p the data pattern $I_{i,p}$, is the value of the input variable from data pattern p in the i dimension, and $C_{i,j}$ is the i dimensional position of cluster j.

Clusters are then assigned data which are closest to them, and the center of each cluster is moved to the centroid of the data associated with that cluster. The revised cluster centers are given by Eq. (6.2)

$$C_{i,j} = \frac{\sum_{p'} I_{i,p'}}{N_{p'}}$$ (6.2)

where $C_{i,j}$ is the i dimensional position of cluster center j, p' the data captured by cluster j, and $N_{p'}$ the number of those captured data.

This process is iterated until equilibrium is reached; i.e. further iterations result in imperceptible changes in the cluster center positions. The cluster membership is established on the basis of the proximity of data to cluster centers: the cluster closest to each datum "captures" that datum as its member.

6.3. RBF CLUSTER RADIUS

The radius of the individual RBF clusters' spheres of influence are determined by the distances between neighboring cluster centers [6,7].

$$\text{RBFdist}(j_1, j_2) = \sqrt{\sum_i (C_{i,j_1} - C_{i,j_2})^2}$$ (6.3)

where $\text{RBFdist}(j_1, j_2)$ is the distance between the centers of clusters j_1 and j_2.

If the nearest two neighbors[28] are used for each cluster, their identification and subsequent use in calculating the cluster's radius is shown in Eq. (6.4).

$$r_{j_1} = \sqrt{\frac{\text{RBFdist}(j_1, j_2)^2 + \text{RBFdist}(j_1, j_3)^2}{2}}$$ (6.4)

---

[28]This approach can be extended to n neighbors if desired. The two-nearest neighbor approach is usually sufficiently robust without adding undue computational burden.

where j_2 and j_3 are the nearest and the second-nearest neighbors, respectively, of cluster j_1.

This important cluster characteristic provides the basis for ascribing a radial Gaussian function to the influence each cluster exerts on the space surrounding it.

$$A_{cp} = \exp(-[D_{pc}]^2/[r_c]^2) \qquad (6.5)$$

where A_{cp} is the activation of any point p in the data space due to cluster c; D_{pc} the distance between data point p and the center of cluster c; and r_c the radius of the hyper-sphere of influence of cluster c.

Eq. (6.5) enables quantification of the degree to which cluster members are associated with the cluster to which they belong. Most importantly, this equation is used to classify fresh conditions or data by identifying which clusters elicit the strongest activation signals from the coordinates describing the new conditions.

In the same manner as indicated in the previous chapter, barring any special needs for focusing on certain regions of the data space, a very simple yet robust pre-processing approach is to compress each input variable linearly into an interval between 0 and 1.

6.4.   COMPETITIVE LEARNING

The principles behind competitive learning were discussed in the section on "unsupervised learning" in Chapter 3. In essence they are based on clusters competing for data members depending on how closely the characteristic fingerprint[29] of the candidate datum corresponds to the cluster's own fingerprint. The following quote from Ref. [1] outlines the essence of auto-classification through competitive learning:

…there is a population of stimulus patterns [each of which] is presented [to the learning system] with some probability. The system is supposed to discover…salient features of the input population. …there is no a priori set of categories into which the patterns are to be classified; rather, the system must develop its own featural representation of the input stimuli which captures the most salient features of the population of input patterns.

---

[29]Defined in Section 2.2.

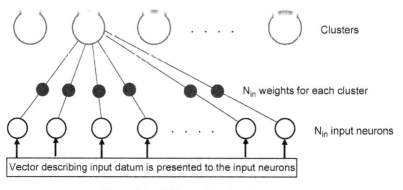

Figure 6.1. Self-organizing learning system.

Figure 6.1 is a schematic representation of a self-organizing system which, as mentioned earlier, incorporates features from competitive learning and adaptive resonance systems, consequently resulting in a very effective structure for industrial application.

The self-organizing, or auto-clustering, process is as follows:

- Input data (each one of which represents a particular N_{in}-dimensional condition) are presented one at a time to the input neurons.
- The cluster whose weights most closely resonate with the input datum vector "captures" that datum.
- The weights of the "capturing" cluster are then adjusted to accommodate this captured datum—this is the unsupervised learning process. The degree of resonance required for capturing data and the learning rate, i.e. extent to which the weights are adjusted, both change with successive learning iterations. The learning rate is decreased and the required degree of resonance is made more stringent as the learning process progresses.
- The learning process continues over a pre-specified number of iterations with pre-specified starting and ending levels of the learning rate and the required resonance.

The weights for each cluster are initially randomized and then normalized in the N_{in} space so that they lie on a hyper-sphere of unit radius:

$$\sqrt{\sum_i w_{ij}^2} = 1 \qquad (6.6)$$

where w_{ij} is the weight connecting input neuron i with cluster j.

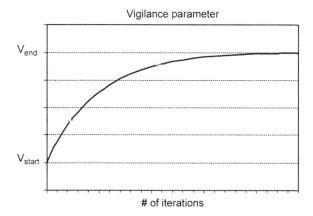

Figure 6.2.   Vigilance parameter increases as auto-clustering proceeds.

The cluster closest in characteristic to a particular input condition, p, is identified by determining which one maximizes the signal:

$$\text{Signal}_j = \sum_i w_{ij} I_{ip} \qquad (6.7)$$

where j denotes the cluster, and I_{ip} is the input value of the ith dimension property of datum p.

Whether or not the condition p is captured by the closest cluster j depends on the degree of resonance (or the similarity) between the weights and the input condition's characteristics. This degree of resonance is quantified by the dot product[30] (defined in Eq. (6.8)) of the cluster's weights and the input datum.

$$\text{Dotproduct}_{wI} = \frac{\sum_i (w_{ij} I_{ip})}{\sqrt{\sum_i w_{ij}^2 \sum_i I_{ip}^2}} \qquad (6.8)$$

The cluster captures the input condition if their dot product equals or exceeds the "vigilance" parameter. This parameter governs the tolerance for dissimilarity within a given cluster. A high tolerance (i.e. low value of vigilance parameter) results in greater dissimilarities between member conditions in each cluster, which correspond to a larger number of member conditions in each cluster and fewer clusters on the whole needed to characterize all the data. The auto-clustering process is started with a low initial value for the vigilance parameter. With each iteration, the value of this parameter is increased until it asymptotically reaches the final pre-specified value as shown in Figure 6.2.

---

[30]The dot product can also be viewed as the multi-dimensional cosine between two vectors.

An algorithm for this asymptotic functional behavior is specified in Eqs. (6.9) and (6.10)

$$V = V_{start} + (1 - e^{-[5(n-1)/N]})(V_{end} - V_{start}) + \Delta \qquad (6.9)$$

where

$$\Delta = V_{end} - (V_{start} + (1 - e^{-[5(N-1)/N]})(V_{end} - V_{start})) \qquad (6.10)$$

where n is the iteration number, and N is the total number of iterations.

If the dot product satisfies the vigilance criterion, and the input datum is captured by the cluster, the cluster's weights are adjusted to accommodate this datum as in Eq. (6.11).

$$\Delta w_{ij} = \eta(\bar{I}_{ip} - w_{ij}) \qquad (6.11)$$

where $\bar{I}_{ip}$ is the input condition normalized on a unit hyper-sphere as in Eq. (6.6) and η is the learning rate.

The learning rate, η, decreases asymptotically with successive iterations between pre-specified starting and ending levels as in Eq. (6.12) and illustrated in Figure 6.3.

$$\eta = \eta_{start} - (1 - e^{-[5(n-1)/N]})(\eta_{start} - \eta_{end}) \qquad (6.12)$$

The learning rate is varied in this manner to allow rapid convergence in the early stages of the learning process, and then minimizing instability by bringing the process into a gentle "landing" at the end.

The weights of the other clusters are left unchanged. In the event that the resonance with the closest cluster is not sufficient to meet the vigilance criterion,

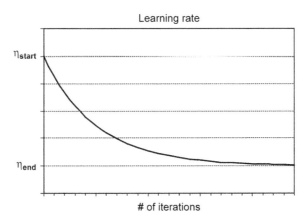

Figure 6.3.　Learning rate decreases as auto-clustering proceeds.

a fresh cluster is initiated to which the input datum is assigned, and the new cluster's weights are set to correspond with the characteristics of its new member.

The maximum permissible number of clusters can be pre-specified if so desired. It may be that not all of these clusters are used if all the data can be accommodated by a smaller number of clusters within the tolerance imposed by the final vigilance level criterion. On the other hand, if this maximum permissible number of clusters cannot accommodate all the data, then the un-accommodated data are so tagged at the end of the process. In this case, the process would have to be repeated either with a larger number of permissible clusters or with a greater tolerance level for cluster membership. Alternatively, there need be no limit imposed on the maximum number of permissible clusters, fresh ones being added as they are needed to accommodate outlying data.

A certain amount of cluster-related book keeping is necessary during the learning process. After the first iteration, a relatively small number of clusters will capture all the data on account of the low initial level of the vigilance parameter. Unused clusters need to be tagged in order that they are available as fresh candidates in future iterations as the progressive tightening of the membership tolerance forces peripheral data out of their earlier cluster assignments.

At the end of every iteration, the weights of each occupied cluster are recalculated to correspond to the centroid of its data membership and then normalized according to Eq. (6.6). If the weight vectors of two or more clusters are similar enough to fall within the vigilance level prevailing for that particular iteration, then the members of these clusters are consolidated into a single new cluster. The weights of this single new cluster are then assigned to correspond to the centroid of its newly consolidated data membership and normalized as in Eq. (6.6), and the recently vacated clusters are tagged as "unused". After such consolidation, the identification of the cluster closest to each individual datum is re-determined. Any disparity in the assignment of data to their closest clusters is corrected by suitable reassignment and resonance check.

6.5. DATA PRE-CONDITIONING FOR COMPETITIVE LEARNING

In Section 6.4, the weights and input data vectors are typically normalized within a hyper-sphere of unit radius (Eq. (6.6)). While this is a very robust default method for pre-conditioning data, there are occasions when it is desirable to use non-normalized "raw" values of the input data and the weight vectors. For example, It Is sometimes of value to visualize, in terms of the actual operating variables, the fingerprint of a cluster's weights superimposed over the fingerprints of its member data, and then use these fingerprints in conjunction with experiential judgment to make strategic or operating decisions. The same procedure and equations from Section 6.4 (except for Eq. (6.6)) can be used for auto-clustering non-normalized data. When doing so it is advisable, though not necessary, that during the process of randomizing the initial weights, for each dimension of every cluster the weights be randomized between the expected minimum and maximum values for that particular dimension.

REFERENCES

[1] Rummelhart, D.E. & McClelland, J.L. Eds. (1986) *Parallel Distributed Processing*, vol. 1, chapter 5, MIT Press, Cambridge, MA.
[2] Kohonen, T. (1989) *Self-Organization and Associative Memory*, 3rd Edition, Springer, Berlin.
[3] Kohonen, T. (2000) *Self-Organization Maps*, 3rd Edition, Springer, Berlin.
[4] Carpenter, G.A. & Grossberg, S. (1988) *Computer*, **21** (3), 77–88.
[5] Carpenter, G.A. & Grossberg, S. (1990) *Neural Networks*, **3**, 129–152.
[6] Moody, J. & Darken, C.J. (1989) *Neural Computation*, **1**, 281–294.
[7] Leonard, J.A. & Kramer, M.A. (1991) *IEEE Control Systems*, April, 31–38.

Chapter 7
Customizing for Industrial Strength Applications

7.1. MODELING: THE QUEST FOR EXPLAINING AND PREDICTING PROCESSES

Modeling aims at capturing the essence of phenomenological behavior. While complete knowledge of reality eludes us, we build models in order to obtain some measure of control over the processes from which we derive profit. Models are never entirely correct[31] but they are useful if they explain and predict phenomeno-logical behavior within the limits of precision required for the task at hand. It is essential that the users of the models understand well the conditions over which the models have been developed and consequently the regimes of their validity.

If the phenomena to be modeled are understood well enough to construct mechanistic models and if their mathematical formulations are amenable to analytical or numerical solution, then the resulting models are very powerful tools as they enable us to explain and predict system behavior very robustly within the bounds of the models' regions of validity. However, as Gershenfeld [1] articulated very aptly:

> The cost for this power is limited applicability—much of the world is simply too complicated to describe this way.

7.2. COMBINING EMPIRICISM WITH MECHANISTIC UNDERSTANDING

The difficulties inherent in constructing mechanistic models are circumvented by developing models directly from observations, i.e. from historical data. This approach presents the developer with its own obstacles, the foremost of which is determining the functional form of the equations used to fit the data. After all, data-driven modeling is most useful when there is inadequate understanding of the underlying principles governing the phenomena being modeled, and so it is far

---

[31]This is an appropriate moment to recall the analogy between models and meticulously crafted watches. While even the most expensive chronometer is *never exactly* correct, it is very useful as it satisfies the needs of its wearer by keeping track of time accurately enough for meeting scheduling requirements. It is amusing to note that a wrist watch that is *exactly* correct is one that has stopped working: such a watch is exactly correct twice each day, but is quite useless as it cannot indicate those two instances in the day when it is telling the time correctly!

from clear what the form of the equations describing the phenomena should be. The advent of neural net technology alleviated this difficulty, enabling the capture of the essential features of complex, non-linear phenomena.

Data-driven models have another problem to be overcome: they do not extrapolate well. In the case of non-linear models extrapolation can occur even within the minimum and maximum bounds of the values of the variables used in training the model. Our vision of an ideal modeling system is one in which the degree of empiricism can be "dialed in". Imagine a rheostat with which the degree of empiricism can be adjusted, depending on the extent of knowledge available: ranging from a completely mechanistic system when the underlying phenomena are well understood to an entirely empirical system when no understanding is available. Such hybrid data-driven models would have engineering judgment or any (albeit partial) understanding, were it available, embedded in them so that their extrapolative capabilities would be enhanced over those afforded by purely empirical models [2].

7.3. EMBEDDING AN IDEALIZED (PARTIALLY CORRECT) MODEL

The concept of enhancing extrapolative performance of a data-driven neural net by embedding a mechanistic model is best illustrated through a simplified example. Let us develop a model to predict the $P-v-T$ behavior of saturated[32] Freon-12. The ideal gas equation of state (which assumes no interactions between the gas molecules) does an excellent job in predicting the behavior of gases at low densities, i.e. at low relative pressure and high relative temperature. Outside this ideal gas region, the ideal gas law breaks down due to the interactions between molecules becoming significant and affecting the behavior of the real gas.

The example chosen here is intentionally trivial in terms of the problem it is addressing in order to focus attention on the modeling concepts. In this example, the model will be required to predict the molar volume[33] of saturated Freon-12 at a given pressure and temperature. A single outcome depends on the values of two parameters. The ideal gas (IG) model for the equation of state is given by

$$\bar{v} = \frac{\bar{R} \cdot T}{P} \tag{7.1}$$

---

[32]That is on its vapor–liquid equilibrium surface.
[33]Molar volume is the inverse of density and has dimensions of volume per mole of gas.

where $\bar{v}$ is the molar volume, T the temperature, P the pressure, and $\bar{R}$ the universal gas constant.

Table 7.1 lists a set of temperatures and pressures along with the corresponding molar volumes for saturated Freon-12. Figure 7.1 shows a parity plot in which the molar volume obtained from ideal gas equation of state is plotted along the ordinate against the actual values of this dependent variable on the abscissa scale. It can be seen that this model predicts the molar volume well at low densities (or high molar volumes), but poorly at high densities.

Let us now train a neural net on a subset of the data in Table 7.1, limiting the range of values of molar volumes over which the neural net is trained so that its extrapolative capability can be effectively tested. Table 7.2 lists the data used to

Table 7.1. F-12 molar volume at different pressures and temperatures

P (kPa)	T (K)	Molar volume (m^3/kmol)
5000	384	0.14
4000	393	0.45
3500	383	0.52
4000	413	0.58
3500	403	0.66
4000	433	0.67
4000	453	0.74
3500	423	0.76
3000	393	0.78
4000	473	0.81
3000	413	0.88
3000	423	0.93
3500	473	0.95
3000	433	0.98
2500	393	1.01
2000	353	1.05
2500	423	1.17
1600	343	1.36
2500	473	1.40
1600	373	1.62
1600	423	1.97
1000	353	2.58
1000	393	3.00
500	323	4.95
500	393	6.28
300	353	9.46
300	383	10.35
100	253	20.28
50	253	41.33

Pattern Recognition in Industry

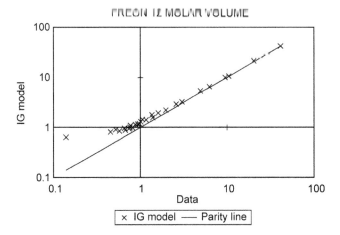

Figure 7.1. Parity plot between real data and the IG model.

Table 7.2. Data used to train neural net

P (kPa)	T (K)	Molar volume $(m^3/kmol)$
4000	393	0.45
4000	413	0.58
4000	433	0.67
4000	453	0.74
4000	473	0.81
3500	383	0.52
3500	403	0.66
3500	423	0.76
3500	473	0.95
3000	423	0.93
2500	393	1.01
2500	423	1.17
2500	473	1.40
1600	343	1.36
1600	373	1.62
1600	423	1.97
1000	353	2.58
1000	393	3.00
500	323	4.95
500	393	6.28
300	353	9.46
300	383	10.35

Table 7.3. Data used to test stand-alone neural net

(a)

P (kPa)	T (K)
5000	384
3000	393
3000	413
3000	433
2000	353
100	253
50	253

(b)

Molar volume (m³/kmol)	Predictions (m³/kmol)
0.14	2.51
0.78	0.99
0.88	0.78
0.98	0.78
1.05	1.55
20.28	3.33
41.33	3.33

train the net. Table 7.3 indicates the data used to test the net. The input data (temperatures and pressures) are shown in Table 7.3a; while Table 7.3b shows the corresponding actual molar volumes and the predicted values. Once trained, the net is used to predict the remaining data points. In the parity plot shown in Figure 7.2 the open squares show how well (or poorly) the neural learned the data on which it was trained, and the open diamonds represent the neural net predictions. The ideal gas model is represented by crosses as in Figure 7.1.

The results are less than desirable. Extrapolation in both the high-density and low-density regions is terrible! For this example we deliberately used very few

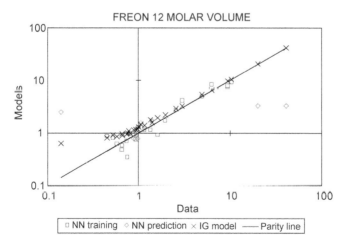

Figure 7.2. Parity plot for stand-alone neural net results.

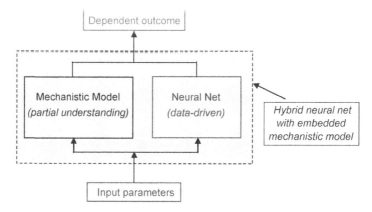

Figure 7.3.   Hybrid combination of partial mechanistic understanding and data-driven model.

training data points and a non-optimal neural net configuration[34] to highlight how an otherwise unsatisfactory data-driven model can be enhanced by embedding mechanistic understanding.

Let us now develop a hybrid combination of a mechanistic model (the ideal gas equation of state, which by itself is not adequate) and a data-driven neural net that compensates for the inaccuracies in the mechanistic model (Figure 7.3). The neural net learns to compensate for deficiencies in the mechanistic understanding by being trained on the discrepancies between the mechanistic model and the actual data. A Radial Basis Function (RBF) structure is often the appropriate architecture for a neural net in this configuration.

The same training data (Table 7.2) is now used to train the neural net in this hybrid combination. The neural net structure deployed in this hybrid is similar to that used earlier: it is an RBF net with two input nodes, one output node, and eight hidden RBF nodes and is, in effect, trained on the discrepancies between the ideal gas model and the real data. In the predictive mode, the output from the neural net is combined with the results of the mechanistic model (the ideal gas equation of state in this case) and the combined outcome is presented as the output from the hybrid model.

In effect, this hybrid model permits the mechanistic understanding to guide the model during extrapolation while the data-driven model "triangulates" within the independent parametric space to correct for the lack of accuracy in the mechanistic understanding.

Table 7.4 shows the prediction results of this hybrid model, and Figure 7.4 illustrates the overall exercise in a graphical parity plot. The filled squares indicate

---

[34]An RBF neural net was used with two input nodes, one output node, and eight RBF hidden nodes.

Table 7.4. Prediction results from hybrid model

(a)   (b)

P (kPa)	T (K)	Molar volume (m³/kmol)	Predictions (m³/kmol)
5000	384	0.14	0.18
3000	393	0.78	0.76
3000	413	0.88	0.90
3000	433	0.98	1.03
2000	353	1.05	1.06
100	253	20.28	20.55
50	253	41.33	41.57

how the hybrid model learned the training data, and the filled diamonds show the results of the hybrid model's predictions for data not used in the training process. Note how very well the hybrid model extrapolates well beyond both the ends of the range of the data used in the training process.

Figure 7.5a and b shows parity plots on a linear scale zooming in to highlight the performance of the hybrid in the "real gas" high-density region where the mechanistic (ideal gas) model loses accuracy.

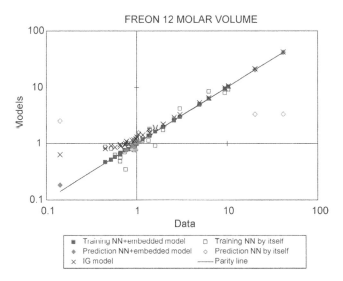

Figure 7.4. Parity plot for overall results.

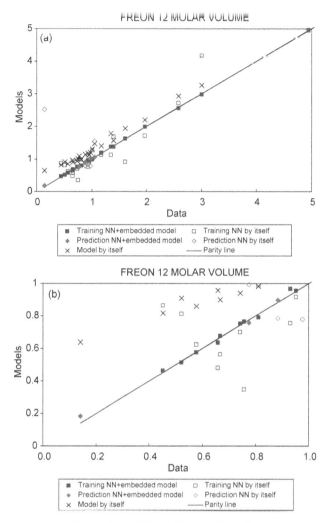

Figure 7.5.   Parity plot for overall results.

7.4.   EMBEDDING A PRIORI UNDERSTANDING IN THE FORM OF CONSTRAINTS

Section 7.3 dealt with embedding a priori mechanistic understanding into data-driven models when it is feasible to articulate that understanding in the form of mathematical equations or logical algorithms. At the other end of the spectrum of articulation, the expression of a priori mechanistic understanding can consist of experience or engineering judgment calls as simple as the specification of directional monotonicity between individual independent variables and the dependent outcomes. Data-driven models developed to describe multi-dimensional, non-linear phenomena extrapolate far more robustly if such monotonic interdependencies exist, are known, and are embedded in the models. The functional form of these interrelationships need not, of course, be specified. Any non-linearities inherent in the phenomena will still be captured by the neural net models as they learn from the data even if the models are constrained according to this type of a priori understanding.

Constraining the behavior of data-driven models is effected by controlling the evolution of the neural nets' weights during the training process. In a back-propagation neural net with one hidden layer as shown in Figure 7.6 if it is known that increasing the value of a particular individual input variable, I, always increases the level of a particular dependent variable, O, then the products of the weights in each connection path between the specific nodes I and O should be greater than zero as in Eq. (7.2)

$$w_{Ij} \cdot w_{jO} > 0 \qquad \text{for all } j \tag{7.2}$$

where w_{ij} is the weight of the connection between neuron i and neuron j.

If at any time during the training process this criterion is not met for one or more of the connection paths between the specific nodes I and O, then the weight, w_{jO}, connecting the hidden neuron, j, to the output neuron, O, in such paths should be reset to zero within that training iteration.

Conversely, if the net is to be constrained such that increasing the value of a particular individual input variable, I, always decreases the level of a particular

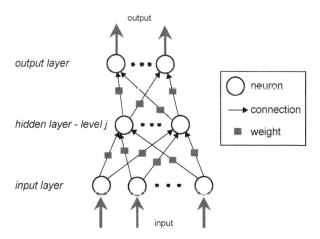

Figure 7.6. Neuron connections in a back-prop net.

dependent variable, O, then the products of the weights in each connection path between the specific nodes I and O should be less than zero as in Eq (7.3)

$$w_{Ij} \cdot w_{jO} < 0 \qquad \text{for all } j \tag{7.3}$$

If the relationship between an individual input variable and a dependent outcome is not known to be monotonic, then the weights in the paths connecting those nodes should be left unconstrained.

It goes without saying that any constraint imposed on a neural net should be consistent with the intrinsic characteristics of the phenomenon being modeled to prevent aberrant model performance. When in doubt it is best either to leave the net unconstrained or, if constrained, to validate its performance by extensively testing its behavior and response to changes in the variables under question. It is not uncommon for a constrained neural net, even if the constraints are well founded, not to converge to the same extent as an unconstrained net, as an unconstrained net is more likely to fit noise in the data.

7.5. INCORPORATING MIXED DATA TYPES

So far in Part II (Technology) of this book the data used to describe the inputs to and outputs from models have been assumed to consist of continuously variable numerals.[35] Let us now consider how to handle data which may take the form of digital or discrete states. As discussed in an earlier chapter in Part I, such data may or may not be amenable to ranking in a seriatim. Variables that can be so ranked are termed *ordinal*, and those which cannot are called *nominal*. An example of an ordinal digital variable is a tertiary switch which assumes one of the three values of increasing rank: "low", "medium", or "high". On the other hand, a nominal digital variable could be a switch that assumes one of n values, each representing one of n states, the effect (on the system being modeled) of any particular state not being in any known ranked order. For example, a business model to predict the cost of an operating process may use as one of its inputs a code identifying a particular vendor.

7.5.1 *Ordinal Digital Variables*
These variables can be conceptually treated very similarly to the way continuously variable numerals are treated. Their effect on the phenomenon being modeled will vary proportionately to their position in their ranked list. The neural net models will

---

[35]Or, what are often referred to in computer terminology as "floating point" numbers.

discern their effect, in conjunction with their interactions with other variables, on the dependent outcome(s). This effect could be non-linear as well as non-monotonic. The difference in implementing their use in models is the way they are scaled in the pre-conditioning process for back-propagation nets.[36] Rather than the procedure described in Section 5.7, they should be scaled so that they are presented in evenly spaced intervals after passing through the sigmoidal squashing function (Figure 5.5).

7.5.2   *Nominal Digital Variables*

As there is no graduated ranking corresponding to the values of nominal variables, it is best to treat them in binary form. There are two approaches in doing this. The first is to create as many binary switches as there are possible values of the nominal variable. In other words, if the nominal variable can take one of the seven values, seven binary (on/off) switches are created. Then to represent the value "3" the third switch would be "on" while the rest were "off". The other approach is to convert the number of possible values (after taking into account that the first value can be represented by 0)[37] into a binary number and have as many switches as the number of digits in that binary number. Each value of the nominal variable is then represented by switching on the binary representation of the value. The latter approach considerably reduces the number of input nodes needed to represent a nominal digital variable. The former approach, however, facilitates interpreting the trained net weight structure[38] to ascertain causal effects of the input variables.

Binary inputs to neural nets need to be scaled so that the signals saturate the neurons to which they are presented. For instance, 0 and 1 need to be presented as -20 and $+20$, respectively[39], to sigmoidal input neurons, so that they elicit a [0,1] response from the neurons.

7.6.   CONFIDENCE MEASURE FOR CHARACTERIZING PREDICTIONS

To know is to have power. Not to know, but knowing when it is that we do not know is also very important. However, it costs us dearly when we do not know, and do not know that we do not know!

---

[36]For RBF nets inputs are best scaled, as always, linearly into the interval [0,1].

[37]As the first value can be represented as 0, a 4-position switch can be represented by two binary digits: the four positions being 00, 01, 10, 11, respectively.

[38]This will be dealt with in more detail in a later chapter.

[39]Or any sufficiently large absolute values, x, that saturate the sigmoidal function: $1/\{1 + \exp(-x)\}$.

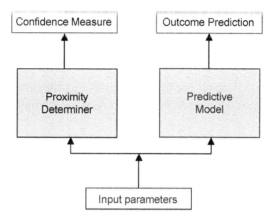

Figure 7.7.   Schematic for processing model predictions.

Hence, it is not enough to develop models that yield answers to questions requested of them. It is very important to know the degree of confidence that can be placed in their answers. Assuming that the models are developed properly, in order to be reliable they need to be exercised within the domain of the data used to create them. As mentioned at an earlier point, non-linear models could be in an extrapolative mode even if the variables prescribing the input condition are within the minimum and maximum levels spanned by the training data.

An effective resolution of this issue is to self-organize the data used to develop the model into multi-dimensional clusters, and then establish the proximity of the input condition, for which a predictive outcome is sought, to the conditions over which the model was trained. Figure 7.7 is a schematic diagram representing this approach. The set of parameters describing the condition, for which a predictive outcome is desired, is used as input to both the predictive model and a proximity determiner. An example of the latter is an RBF auto-clustering model[40] which has, through unsupervised learning, clustered all the previously encountered experiential data used to develop the predictive model. This RBF model can now quantify the proximity of the fresh input condition to the nearest cluster in the data space comprising previous experience, and so provide a measure of confidence in the predictive model's answer.

The distance between the fresh input condition and either the nearest historical datum or nearest cluster center is the basis on which the metric for the confidence measure is established. A non-linear function that penalizes distance from

---

[40]Described in Sections 6.2 and 6.3.

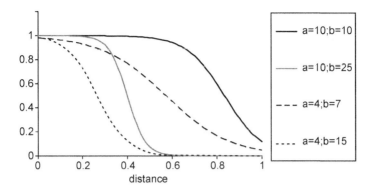

Figure 7.8. Function for confidence measure (Eq. (7.4)).

the nearest historical datum or cluster center is used to characterize the extent of potential extrapolation. Eq. (7.4) suggests such a function, the evaluation of which drops of as the distance from the focal point (i.e. historical datum or cluster center) increases. This function provides a penalty-free zone around the focal point. The radius of this penalty-free zone and the slope of the subsequent drop-off can be controlled by the choice of parameters *a* and *b*, as shown in Figure 7.8.

$$f = 1 - \frac{1}{(1 + \exp\{a - b\cdot\text{dist}\})} \tag{7.4}$$

7.7. INTERPRETING TRAINED NEURAL NET STRUCTURES

Model users are justifiably averse to "black boxes". When using models in making decisions or developing strategies, decision makers derive comfort from the perception of control over, and understanding of, what is "inside" the model and how the results are arrived at. Over the years, higher education in engineering and the sciences has ingrained in the professional community the notion of comfort in dealing with explicitly expressed models. As a consequence, there is considerable resistance to, and at times an almost visceral reaction against, using models that may appear as "black boxes". It is, therefore, imperative that the "black box" syndrome be alleviated in the development of powerful, non-linear data-driven models so that, through their acceptance, they may be put to profitable use.

Insight into a neural net's behavior can be attained by interpreting the structure of the net's weights. The "causal indices" relating the independent variables to their dependent outcomes can be deduced from the weights [3]. These causal indices are determined by considering the weights in the paths between individual input and output nodes. This concept is very similar to that espoused in Section 7.4. The causal index, C_{IO}, relating output O to input I is given by:

$$C_{IO} = \sum_j w_{Ij} \cdot w_{jO} \qquad (7.5)$$

the summation being over all the paths between I and O through all the hidden nodes j.

A large positive value for the index as determined by Eq. (7.5) would indicate that output O is strongly dependent on input I, increasing as I increases. Conversely, a large negative causal index indicates strong negative monotonic dependency. The degree to which different input variables influence the dependent outcome is discerned by the relative values of their causal indices. This, however, only holds for monotonic relationships. A strong non-monotonic dependency would result in a low value for the causal index, as would a weak dependency. Absolute causal indices, as shown in Eq. (7.6), are needed to distinguish between these two very different types of relationships which exhibit similar levels of relative causal indices

$$\text{Abs } C_{IO} = \sum_j |w_{Ij}| \cdot |w_{jO}| \qquad (7.6)$$

summed over all the paths between I and O through all the hidden nodes j.

Interpreting the behavior of the neural net model is accomplished by examining the indices obtained through Eqs. (7.5) and (7.6). Large positive or negative values of the relative causal index (Eq. (7.5)) imply a strongly influential monotonic relationship between the independent variable and the dependent outcome. Low values of Eq. (7.5) result from either weak dependency or non-monotonic behavior. If, however, there is strong non-monotonic dependency, the absolute causal index (Eq. (7.6)) would be large even though the relative index is small. A very weak relationship between the independent and dependent variables is detected by low values of both relative and absolute causal indices.

Let us illustrate this method of dissecting a neural net through a very simple, contrived example. We will train a neural net with four input variables and a single outcome. The outcome will be separately calculated as the result of a function, shown in Eq. (7.7), depending on three input variables. An additional input furnished to the net will have no effect on the outcome

$$f = \frac{10x - 5x^2 + 2y}{z} \tag{7.7}$$

The function is strongly and non-monotonically dependent on x, strongly negatively dependent on z, and less strongly dependent on y with positive monotonicity. A neural net, shown in Figure 7.9, was trained on data in the following manner. Variables 1, 2, and 4 represented x, y, and z, respectively, in Eq. (7.7) and were randomly assigned, and were used to generate corresponding values for f as in Eq. (7.7) which were then used as target outcomes to train the net. Variable 3 was also randomly assigned, and had no effect on the output on which the net was trained.

Figure 7.10a and b shows the causal indices obtained from the trained net's weights.

The first striking observation from inspecting the causal indices is that variable 3 can be seen to have no effect on the outcome. Variable 1 clearly has a strong impact on the outcome based on its high absolute causal index (Figure 7.10b),

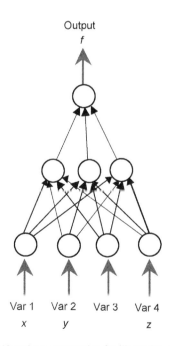

Figure 7.9. Neural net construction for illustrating causal indices.

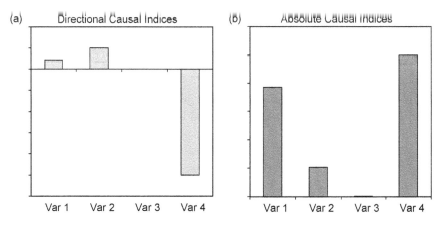

Figure 7.10. Causal indices.

which taken in tandem with the low directional causal index value (Figure 7.10a) indicates that its effect is non-monotonic. The causal indices for variable 4 show it to have a strong monotonically negative effect on the outcome, whereas in the case of variable 2 similar moderate causal indices in both figures indicate a moderate positive monotonic influence on the outcome.

7.8. GRAPHICAL INTERPRETATION OF TRAINED NEURAL NET STRUCTURES

The behavior of neural net models can also be very effectively ascertained by visualizing effects of individual input variables on the outcome(s). The world we inhabit restricts us to displaying results on two-dimensional surfaces, and so we are constrained in our ability to view such effects. However, with some degree of ingenuity this limitation can be surmounted reasonably effectively.

A simple and effective method for visualizing a neural net model's behavior is to construct an automated template in which the predictive model can be exercised to show the effect of individual inputs while holding the values of the other inputs at pre-selected levels. For the same example used in Section 7.7, Figure 7.11a–d shows the effects of each of the four variables on the net output over the range of their training data while the other variables are kept at their mean training levels.

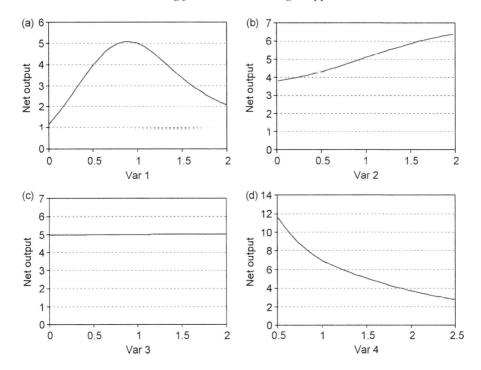

Figure 7.11. (a) Neural net response to variable 1. (b) Neural net response to variable 2. (c) Neural net response to variable 3. (d) Neural net response to variable 4.

REFERENCES

[1] Gershenfeld, N. (1999) *The Nature of Mathematical Modeling*, Cambridge University Press, Cambridge.
[2] Kramer, M.A., Thompson, M.L. & Bhagat, P.M. (1992) *Embedding Theoretical Models in Neural Networks*, American Control Conference, Chicago.
[3] Baba, K., Enbutu, I. & Yoda, M. (1990) *Explicit Representation of Knowledge Acquired from Plant Historical Data Using Neural Network*, IJCNN-90, Washington, DC, June 1990.

Chapter 8

Characterizing and Classifying Textual Material

This chapter describes automation of the process of reading and classifying text documents using pattern recognition technology; thereby enabling very rapid scanning of business, technical, patent, and trade literature in order to identify competitive trends and strategies.

8.1. CAPTURING A DOCUMENT'S ESSENTIAL FEATURES THROUGH FINGERPRINTING

The first question one asks about a document in order to determine its value is: "What is it about?" Translating this question to pose it to an automated system led to the development of the process of "fingerprinting" a document so as to capture its essential features. Such a fingerprint is composed of the frequencies with which certain words or terms occur in the document. Consequently, in mathematical terms a document is represented by a vector in a multi-dimensional space, the dimensions of which incorporate the occurrence frequencies of the context words or terms. Several hundreds or thousands of words or terms may be used to define this contextual space depending on the particular interests of the user.

The encapsulation of a document into a single multi-element vector permits the quantification of similarities between different documents. This is done by examining the dot product of the document vectors. As discussed in earlier chapters, this dot product[41] of two vectors is a measure of the angular distance between them: a dot product of zero means that the vectors are orthogonal (i.e. the documents are totally different); a dot product of unity indicates that the vectors are exactly parallel (or that the documents are similar). The dot product, which is a single number, is a very effective and simple measure of similarity in situations described by a very large number of dimensions.

---

[41]or multi-dimensional cosine.

8.2.   SIMILAR DOCUMENTS AUTO-CLASSIFIED INTO DISTINCT CLUSTERS

If the answer to our first question "What is the document about?" suggests that the document is about something interesting or potentially valuable, a host of secondary questions then spring to mind such as: "Which other documents relate to this one?"; "How does this document differ from others in the same area?"; "How can groups of documents dealing with similar subject matter be identified and organized?"; and so on. The quantitative description of a document (given by its fingerprint, or characteristic vector) coupled with pattern recognition technology provide the means with which these questions can be addressed.

Self-organization architectures can auto-classify large numbers (several thousands) of text documents by identifying clusters of documents in which members share common fingerprint patterns [1]. This technique permits the desired degree of similarity between documents to be specified for being associated with each other as members of a particular cluster. In other words, the selectivity with which clusters of documents accept or reject new members can be controlled. Specifying a narrower tolerance (or a higher level of selectivity) leads to greater similarity between members in a given cluster and, consequently, fewer members per cluster. This training process has been described in Section 3.3, and the technical details have been described in Section 6.4; the schematic diagram is shown in Figure 8.1.

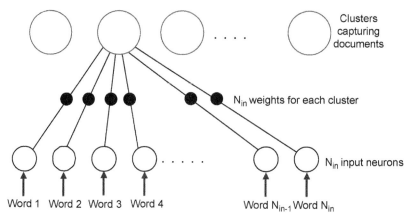

Figure 8.1.   Schematic diagram for auto-classifying documents.

Just as an individual document can be characterized by a fingerprint or vector, so also can a cluster be represented by its fingerprint. Hence, the degree to which a particular cluster resembles other clusters can be quantified by the dot product of the clusters' vectors. A cluster's fingerprint or vector serves to describe the common features of its member documents. As these clusters evolve by self-selection in a training process, they are not constrained by any rigid predetermined categorical boundaries and, therefore, are not subject to preconceived notions. On the other hand, should the user have well-defined objectives in mind for seeking or cataloging information, this pattern recognition technology can be guided in its definition of the clusters' profiles.

The clusters are formed through an automated training process in which documents are grouped together based on the similarities between their fingerprint patterns. In the early stages of training, the selectivity level is kept low. This yields a coarse initial classification comprehensively encompassing all or most of the documents under investigation. The training continues iteratively with progressively increasing selectivity until the desired selectivity is asymptotically reached. The result of this training is the identification and formation of distinct clusters containing member documents sharing common features. Documents exhibiting no similarity with any other document (within the specified selectivity tolerance) would be identified as outliers and would not have any "fellow members."

8.3. ACTIVITY PROFILES OF AUTHORS PROVIDE COMPETITIVE INSIGHT

The fingerprinting and vectoring methodology can be extended to capture the activity profiles of authors and inventors. In the same way in which clusters' fingerprints describe the common features of their member documents, so also can the fingerprints of each author's documents or inventor's patents be melded into a composite fingerprint characterizing the activity profile of that author or inventor. The most prolific authors or inventors in a given field or organization can be identified along with their activity profiles. As in forensic fingerprint matching, the activity profiles of authors and inventors in a given field can rapidly be scanned and evaluated on the basis of their quantitative similarity to a given activity template. Recognizing similarities in patterns between the activity profiles of prolific authors and inventors can identify groups of collaborators working in areas of interest. The history and evolution of such groups gives insight into how resources are being deployed in the industry and how strategies are changing with time. Conversely, the fingerprint of a cluster representing a technology of interest serves as a template to identify key individuals working in that area. This is done by invoking the individuals' activity profiles and quantitatively determining their similarities with the template fingerprint.

8.4.   VISUALIZING A DOCUMENT'S CONTENTS

A picture is worth a thousand words. Which over-worked engineer or manager has not wished that the concepts embedded in a document be transported instantly into his or her brain? The challenge lies in being able to represent the contents of a document by an easily absorbed image. Having quantified the document by a fingerprint gives us the capability of meeting this challenge. We are used to grasping the properties of a compound by looking at a spectral analysis diagram such as an IR spectral diagram or a gas chromatogram. The same format can be used to display the fingerprint of a document, cluster or activity profile. Further, simultaneous display of two (or more) such entities would enable swift pattern recognition at the human brain level; after all, our brains have several hundred billion neurons compared to the relatively very few used in artificial neural nets. The next issue to be attended to is the large dimensionality of the fingerprint. This is more easily addressed when it is realized that any given document or profile is likely to occupy a relatively sparse band within the total number of dimensions permitted to the vector, and, more importantly, a filter for "zooming" in on the more significant dimensions (i.e. those with larger magnitudes) easily enables succeeding views of different levels of detail. A rather trivial example of the key features of a specific patent and the cluster to which it belongs is shown in Figure 8.2 to illustrate the idea.

Such an image is invoked on selecting a particular document from a list of documents in a given area. Further exploration enables the examination of the cluster and the invocation of a list of all other documents captured by that

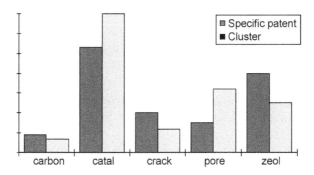

Figure 8.2.   Visualizing a document's key features.

cluster. The growth (or decline) of the activity represented by that cluster over a period of time is easily viewed. The activity profile of an author or inventor may similarly be viewed. Many different investigative paths may be followed to identify critical areas or individuals. For example, ranked lists of authors can be compiled by quantifying the similarities of their activity profiles with the activity of a known prolific or influential individual. Another investigative trail could originate by invoking the clusters dealing with a given area of interest, decomposing those clusters into their member documents, identifying activity profiles of the authors, identifying their respective co-workers, and then branching out to examine related areas these individuals are involved in.

A bird's eye view of several thousand documents or patents is obtained easily and very rapidly: by viewing the prominent features of the documents or patents; viewing and identifying selected or important cluster areas; and viewing the activity profiles of key individuals and identifying their co-workers.

8.5. IDENTIFYING KEYWORDS THROUGH ENTROPIC ANALYSIS OF TEXT DOCUMENTS

The technology expounded thus requires as input a list of keywords or root terms which make up the operating spatial dimensions. While it is easy to specify unique terms of interest, the real challenge lies in determining key terms that characterize each of thousands of documents whose nature or even relevance is not known at the outset. The essential issue here is to distinguish those words that are commonly used parts of speech from the words that carry significant information characterizing the documents' content.

The thermodynamic concept of entropy enables us to scrutinize all the documents to be analyzed and automate the extraction of information-rich words from the rest [2]. Information entropy is a property that encapsulates the nature of how words are distributed throughout the documents. Quoting from Ref. [2]:

> Without assuming any previous knowledge of the syntactic structure of language, we are able to cluster certain groups of words according to their specific role in the text.

The central idea is that the distribution probabilities of different words yield insight into the type of information conveyed by them. We will now develop the methodology for quantitative analysis. Some definitions follow:

$M \equiv$ total number of documents we intend to analyze;
$N_d \equiv$ the number of words in document d;

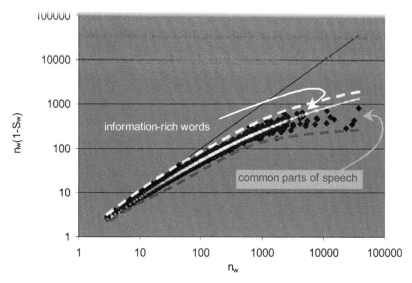

Figure 8.3.   Entropy map of all the words in a collection of documents.

$n_{wd} \equiv$ the frequency[42] with which word w occurs in document d;

$f_{wd} \equiv n_{wd}/N_d$;

$p_{wd} \equiv f_{wd}/\sum_{d=1}^{M} f_{wd}$ where the summation is over M, i.e. over all the documents;

$n_w \equiv$ the frequency of occurrence of word w in all M documents $= \sum_{d=1}^{M} n_{wd}$.

The entropy, S_w, of word w is then defined as:

$$S_w = -\frac{1}{\ln(M)} \sum_{d=1}^{M} \{p_{wd} \ln (p_{wd})\} \tag{8.1}$$

The physical significance of the entropy of a word is that uniform distribution of a word in a large number of documents will result in a higher entropy value for that word than in the case of words that are selectively clustered in only a few documents. In the limit, the entropy of a word that appears in a single document is zero; there being no uncertainty as to where to find that particular word.

Figure 8.3 shows an entropy map for all the words in a collection of documents. Each word is represented by a solid diamond. The frequency of occurrence of each word in all the documents, n_w, is plotted on the abscissa; the ordinate shows the word's negentropy taking into account its frequency of use. Words with zero entropy would occupy a position on the parity line. Information-rich words are at the upper end of the word band, and can be identified by skimming off the top of this band.

---

[42]In other words, the number of times word w occurs in document d.

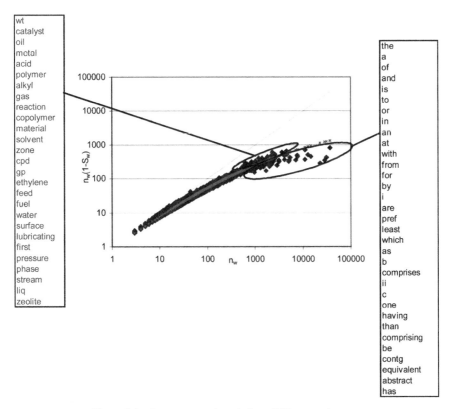

Figure 8.4. Entropy map of words from 3000 patent abstracts.

To demonstrate this approach, approximately 3000 patent abstracts relating to the petrochemical industry were analyzed with this technology. Figure 8.4 shows sample words obtained from a top-skim as well as from a bottom-skim of the word band. The results speak for themselves.

The documents analyzed in this example were abstracts and so contained a high density of key terms, therefore resulting in the relatively thin word band seen in these figures. Nonetheless, skimming from the top of the band yields a list of information-rich words with which the dimensional space (for subsequent fingerprinting, auto-clustering and visualizing) can be constructed.

A final word is in order to facilitate top-skimming from the word band consisting of thousands of word points. A Hoerl function[43] is used to fit the word points in a log–log entropy map. Its position within the word band is then suitably

---

[43]The Hoerl function: $y = ax^b \exp(cx)$ is a very powerful 3-parameter function for fitting 2D data.

adjusted depending on the nature of the documents under analysis, and the word points above it are harvested to constitute the dimensional space.

8.6.   AUTOMATION SHRINKS TIME AND RESOURCES REQUIRED TO KEEP UP WITH THE WORLD

Today's environment demands high productivity and a comprehensive knowledge of ones competitive position under conditions of shrinking budgets and resource pools. A few thousand documents would require a small army of individuals many months to read, to weed out the unimportant ones, and to categorize the rest. These consultants would also bring, along with their expertise, their preconceptions. By contrast, an automated competitive intelligence system such as the one described in this chapter could read and organize the same number of documents in a matter of a few hours. The results of the automated execution are amenable to a wide range of rapid analyses, in addition to enabling instantaneous graphical representation of the documents, their relationships to one another, the activity profiles of the authors and their collaborative groups, and the competition's strategy.

This new technology enables organizations to digest enormous amounts of information rapidly and efficiently. Furthermore, when implemented on-line it is able to scan current news and literature items and alert management on changes in markets and competitors' strategies. It could significantly impact the way in which businesses keep their competitive edge.

REFERENCES

[1] Salton, G. (1988) *Automatic Text Processing*, Addison-Wesley, Reading, MA.
[2] Montemurro, M.A. & Zanette, D.H. (2001) *Entropic Analysis of the Role of Words in Literary Texts*, eprint arXiv:cond-mat/0109218, September 2001.

Chapter 9

Pattern Recognition in Time Series Analysis

9.1. LEADING INDICES AS DRIVERS

Predicting the future by analyzing the past has been an ever-consuming human desire. The quest for its realization has engaged, amongst others, mathematicians, scientists, engineers, and economists for decades, yielding rich mathematical and methodological bounties. As with modeling in general, if mechanistic understanding of the governing phenomena is available, then, in principle, future behavior can be predicted through the formulation and solution of the underlying deterministic equations. If such understanding is absent, as is often the case, future behavior needs to be inferred by examining the patterns of the past. Two schools of thought exist in approaching this undertaking. The first espouses the notion that predicting future behavior requires identifying and taking into account the effects of other leading indicators, or drivers. The second believes that all the information pertaining to the phenomenon is embedded in the past behavior of the index itself, and so its future performance can be predicted independently of other factors; and an excellent source of reference for this is Ref. [1]. In the present book however, we will exclusively address the cause-and-effect approach: dealing with identifying and subsequently harnessing the behavior of one or more leading indices that govern and drive the index of interest to be predicted.

9.2. CONCEPT OF RESONANCE IN QUANTIFYING SIMILARITIES BETWEEN TIME SERIES

What are the features shared between two time series that enable us to determine the degree to which they are similar? For our ultimate purpose of identifying potential leading indicators, this question is qualitatively answered as follows: "To the extent that the series move up and down in tandem". Another way of expressing this is by asking whether they resonate, or are "in sync", with each other. The degree of resonance between them is quantitatively determined by their *dot product*.

Let us consider two time series: x_t and y_t, where $t = 1, 2, 3, ..., T$. Eq. (9.1) expresses the degree of resonance, R_{xy}, between them

$$R_{xy} = \frac{\sum_{t=1}^{T}\{(x_t - \mu_x)\cdot(y_t - \mu_y)\}}{\sqrt{\sum_{t=1}^{T}(x_t - \mu_x)^2} \cdot \sqrt{\sum_{t=1}^{T}(y_t - \mu_y)^2}} \tag{9.1}$$

where

$$\mu_x = \frac{\sum_{t=1}^{T}x_t}{T}, \quad \text{and} \quad \mu_y = \frac{\sum_{t=1}^{T}y_t}{T}$$

R_{xy} equals 1 for series that resonate perfectly. Of equal interest to us are series that resonate in a contrary manner, i.e. those that are vertical mirror images of each another. In the case of exact contrary resonance, R_{xy}, as determined by Eq. (9.1), is equal to -1. The degree of resonance (or contrary resonance) increases as the absolute value of R_{xy} approaches unity. Very small absolute values of R_{xy} correspond to series that bear little resemblance to each other.

9.3. IDENTIFYING LEADING INDICATORS

Leading indicators are identified by searching for indices whose time series resonate strongly with that of the index which is to be predicted. It is, of course, not of much use if this resonance is concurrent or lags; rather, it needs to lead sufficiently in order to enable forecasting with the desired anticipatory time interval.

The method that we have developed for successfully identifying leading indicators is to cut "snippets" of the candidate index and the index of interest covering time spans over which we believe existing conditions to prevail, and then slide the candidate snippet forward in time until maximum resonance between the two series is obtained as shown in Figures 9.1 and 9.2. In Figure 9.1 the leading indicator candidate, series x, is shown by the dashed line, and the series of interest, y, by the solid line.

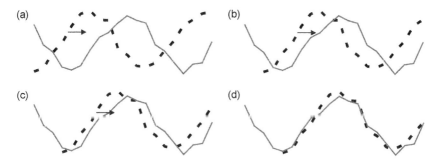

Figure 9.1. Sliding the candidate "snippet" forward for maximum resonance.

As the candidate series x is slid forward by a lead interval L, the resonance between x and the series to be predicted, y, is given by Eq. (9.2)

$$R_{x(t-L),y(t)} = \frac{\sum_{t=1}^{T}\{(x_{t-L} - \mu_x)\cdot(y_t - \mu_y)\}}{\sqrt{\sum_{t=1}^{T}(x_{t-L} - \mu_x)^2} \cdot \sqrt{\sum_{t=1}^{T}(y_t - \mu_y)^2}} \quad (9.2)$$

where

$$\mu_x = \frac{\sum_{t=1-L}^{T-L} x_t}{T}, \qquad \text{and} \qquad \mu_y = \frac{\sum_{t=1}^{T} y_t}{T}$$

The series x is clearly a leading indicator of series y with a lead interval corresponding to (d) in Figure 9.2.

The process of screening a large number of candidate leading indicators can be automated using Eq. (9.2) and specifying the snippet length, T, and maximum and minimum bounds for the lead interval, L. The snippet length is chosen on the basis

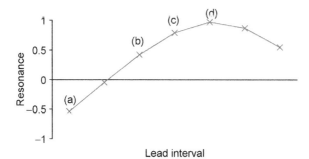

Figure 9.2. Resonance as the candidate "snippet" slides forward.

of the domain time span over which there is reasonable confidence that the prevailing conditions remain the same and represent the environment in which predictions are desired. The minimum lead time is determined by the desired advance prediction time interval. A maximum lead interval also needs to be specified to form a time boundary beyond which it is unreasonable to expect a cause-and-effect relationship.

It is often instructive to view graphically the superposed series involving promising candidates at different lead time intervals. Viewing is facilitated by normalizing each series: mean centering and attenuating each element by the standard deviation as in Eq. (9.3)

$$\hat{x}_t = \frac{x_t - \mu_x}{\sigma_x} \tag{9.3}$$

where

$$\mu_x = \frac{\sum_{t=1}^{T} x_t}{T}, \quad \text{and} \quad \sigma_x = \frac{\sqrt{\sum_{t=1}^{T}(x_t - \mu_x)^2}}{T - 1}$$

9.4. FORECASTING

Adaptive learning neural net models are constructed to correlate the index of interest at time t with identified drivers, or leading indicators, each of which is presented with its appropriate lead interval based on maximizing its resonance with the target index to be predicted (Figure 9.3).

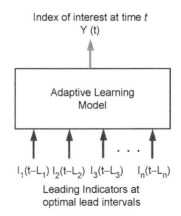

Figure 9.3.   Neural net model correlates index of interest with leading indicators.

The model is trained on historical data: each datum being taken at one point in time, with each leading indicator being displaced by the interval at which its series has maximum resonance with the target series.

In many cases it is advisable to deal with *changes* in the index from the previous time step rather than the index itself. The driving indices are then chosen by examining the resonance of the series of their changes with the series of changes of the target index. It is often more important to predict the direction and trend of an index rather than its level. Furthermore, models to predict changes (or percentage change) are more sensitive to detecting underlying features in the time series behavior.

REFERENCE

[1] Weigend, A.S. & Gershenfeld, N.A. Eds. (1994) *Time Series Prediction*, Proceedings Volume XV, Santa Fe Institute Studies in the Sciences of Complexity.

Chapter 10
Genetic Algorithms

10.1. BACKGROUND

Genetic algorithms were discussed qualitatively in Section 3.5. Genetic algorithms incorporate natural selection principles from evolutionary biology into a stochastic framework, resulting in a very powerful optimizing methodology. They are especially well suited for optimizing highly non-linear multi-dimensional phenomena which pose considerable difficulty to conventional methods particularly if the objective functions to be optimized are discontinuous and/or non-monotonic. One of the main advantages of using genetic algorithms is that they are not trapped by local optima.

Genetic algorithms (GAs) differ from conventional stochastic optimization techniques (such as simulated annealing) in that they are driven towards convergence by principles of natural selection. Simulated genes encode values of the independent parameters that describe the operating conditions. A set of these genes constitute a chromosome, which has an associated relative "fitness" with respect to the objective functions to be optimized depending on the values of the independent parameters (or genes). A set of independent parameters is "fitter" than another set if it yields a better (i.e. more optimal) value of the objective functions.

This approach was conceived by John Holland at The University of Michigan, and his first monograph on the subject, published in 1975 [1], hardly received the attention that should have been accorded to such a creative and powerful "invention". His students kept the flame smoldering, and in 1989 one of them wrote a "definitive" text on the subject [3]. By that time there was an exponential increase in the number of researchers exploring and mining this very rich vein, and now the literature is filled with research papers, conference proceedings, and examples of genetic algorithms being applied to areas ranging from the engineering sciences to finance.

What is interesting, however, is that in much of the literature genetic algorithms are deployed so as to operate on binary genes. In other words, binary strings are used to express the variables that are to be optimized. Though this may facilitate implementation of the original GA scheme, it focuses unequal attention on different variables if varying degrees of precision are used in their expression. This chapter will expound genetic algorithms that operate upon continuous variables (e.g. floating point numbers) as individual genes. Furthermore, in our GA methodology, individual genes may also be expressed as multi position switches. In their simplest form such switches are binary (i.e. on or off); but they can also have a number of discrete (and not necessarily sequential or ordinal[44]) positions, e.g. representing a set of any number of different conditions or alternatives. In order to realize this capability, we have developed novel techniques for the mutation and mating (cross-over) processes.

10.2. DEFINITIONS

Simply stated, the problem that a GA solves is finding the values (or sets of values) of a set of variables, $v_1, v_2, \ldots, v_n$, that maximize a given objective function $f(v_1, v_2, \ldots, v_n)$.

Each *gene* is defined as a variable, e.g. v_m, the value of which is to be optimized. A *chromosome* is a set of genes which is used to evaluate the pre-specified objective function (Figure 10.1).

The *fitness* of a chromosome is the value of the objective function calculated by using the values of the genes of which the chromosome is constituted (Figure 10.2).

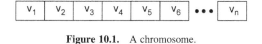

Figure 10.1.   A chromosome.

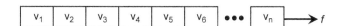

Figure 10.2.   The fitness of a chromosome.

10.3. SETTING THE STAGE

An initial population of chromosomes (Figure 10.3) is generated with randomized values for each gene in every chromosome. The boundaries of the *n*-dimensional variable space being explored by the GA are set by randomizing each gene's

---

[44]i.e. rankable.

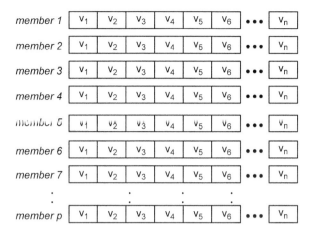

Figure 10.3. Initial chromosome population.

value between the minimum and maximum levels to be considered for the variable being represented by that gene.

The fitness (i.e. value of the objective function) for each chromosome is then calculated (Figure 10.4).

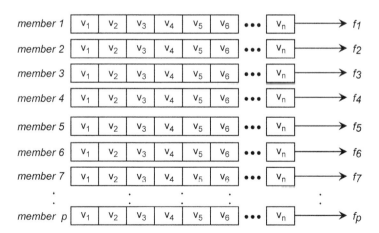

Figure 10.4. Fitness calculated for each chromosome.

10.4. SELECTION

The first step in selecting members of the next generation of chromosomes consists of constructing a stochastic roulette wheel in which each chromosome is represented by a segment in the wheel. The size of each segment is related to the fitness of the chromosome. Fitter chromosomes are represented by large segments; "thin" segments represent less fit chromosomes (Figure 10.5). Spinning such a weighted roulette wheel results in a higher probability for selecting fitter chromosomes over those not as fit. It is important to note that it is not just the very fittest chromosomes that are chosen de facto. Diversity is not merely politically correct; it is seen to lead ultimately to very fit overall populations (or solutions in the case of GAs).

This weighted roulette wheel is then "spun" stochastically as many times as the number of members (or chromosomes) desired to populate the next generation. Choosing multiple copies of the same chromosome is permitted should that occur stochastically.

To select each member of the new generation, the sum of the fitness functions, Σ_f, for all the members of the previous generation is first calculated (Eq. (10.1)):

$$\Sigma_f = \sum_j f_j \qquad (10.1)$$

A position, P_Σ, within the roulette wheel is selected randomly as in Eq. (10.2):

$$P_\Sigma = r\Sigma_f \qquad (10.2)$$

where r is a random number in the interval $[0,1]$.

The individual member corresponding to this selected position is identified by looping through the population while at the same time summing up the

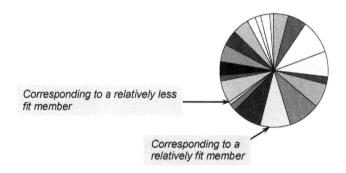

Corresponding to a relatively less fit member

Corresponding to a relatively fit member

Figure 10.5. Weighted roulette wheel.

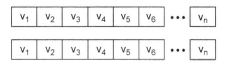

Figure 10.6. Selected pair of chromosomes.

fitness functions of the members individually; keeping track of this running sum and stopping at the particular member when the running sum corresponds to P_Σ.

Up to this point in the evolutionary process, there has been no improvement in the best chromosome's fitness (or in the best solution to the optimization problem). We have merely chosen samples from the initial pool of chromosomes with randomized genes. It is time, therefore, to move on to the next step.

10.5. MATING

The chromosomes selected as candidates for the next generation are randomly paired together as "parents" (Figure 10.6).

The genes from each "parent" are identified (Figure 10.7).

The mating process (also called "cross-over") is then accomplished by creating daughters from the parents by randomly crossing over genes between the chromosomes (Figure 10.8).

The probability of any gene crossing over is pre-specified. A cross-over probability of 0.5 would result, on average, in each daughter's chromosome containing 50% of the genes from each parent. The results of cross-over probabilities other than 0.5 are symmetrical on either side of 0.5: cross-over probabilities of 0.2 and 0.8 both result in a 20–80% split of genes from the parents in the daughters; i.e. on average one daughter will have 20% of one parent's genes and 80% of the genes from the other parent. While the best cross-over probability for a particular problem depends on the nature of the problem, a default value of 0.2 is usually a good starting point to use.

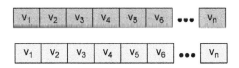

Figure 10.7. Genes from each parent identified.

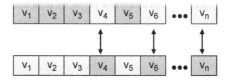

Figure 10.8.   Daughters created by randomly crossing over genes.

As we all know, there is no guarantee that daughters are any better than their parents! At this point, then, we are ready for yet another feature in the evolutionary process.

10.6.   MUTATION

Genes are given the opportunity to mutate as each new daughter is created. In the conventional binary gene GA, this was accomplished by changing a 0 into a 1 (and vice versa) with a pre-specified probability. In our case genes can be continuous variables. Therefore, mutation takes a different form. Genes can be "perturbed" from their existing values to different extents with varying probability (Figure 10.9).

Large perturbations in gene values are allowed to occur infrequently; smaller perturbations to occur more frequently while, at a pre-specified probability level, some genes are undisturbed.

In the case of those genes representing multi-position switches, mutation takes the form of the gene value being switched randomly to another position at a pre-specified probability level.

A continuous probability function as shown in Figure 10.9 carries with it unnecessary computational expense as we have found that a stepped function as

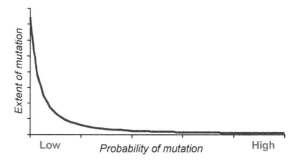

Figure 10.9.   Floating-point gene mutation.

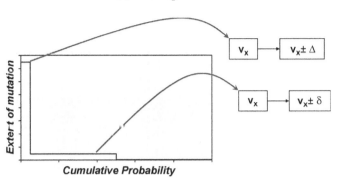

Figure 10.10. "Stepped" floating-point gene mutation.

shown in Figure 10.10 is still very effective while requiring reduced computational overhead. The number of steps and the extent of mutational change at each step can be customized to meet the needs of the problem being solved. The extent of mutation does not imply an invariant mutational change. Rather, it specifies the maximum allowable change associated with a given probability of occurrence; the actual change being randomly effected within this allowable limit.

During the cross-over process, while each daughter's chromosome is being assembled from the parents' chromosomes, each gene is considered as a target for mutation. If we adopt a three-step mutation model as shown in Figure 10.10, then with a low probability (p_1) the gene's value is changed randomly between the minimum and maximum bounds set for the variable corresponding to that gene. With a somewhat higher probability (p_2) the gene is changed to a value randomly chosen within a (small) preset interval, δ, on either side of its current value. With probability ($1 - p_1 - p_2$) the gene is left unchanged.

Mutation of variables that are represented by switches rather than numerical values is effected by allowing the switch to assume any one of its permissible settings randomly. For example, a variable represented by an n-position switch would mutate with probability[45] (p_m) by assuming any one of its n possible settings with probability $1/n$.

Suitable values of p_1, p_2, δ, and p_m are obtained by tuning them so that they are appropriate for the problem being solved. Default candidate values[46] with which to start the tuning process are 0.04, 0.5, 10%, and 0.3, respectively.

---

[45]p_m is the preset level of mutation probability.

[46]These default suggestions are just that. The idiosyncrasies of each particular problem such as the number of variables, their range, and the complexity and nature of the objective function require judicious customization of these factors.

10.7. "BREEDING" FIT SOLUTIONS

The next generation of chromosomes is evolved by combining the selection, mating, and mutation operations (Figure 10.11).

This evolutionary process is repeated until chromosomes corresponding to very fit solutions are obtained (Figure 10.12).

In the preface to the later edition of his monograph [2], Holland noted the following initial reaction to his concept of GA:

> Why would somebody study learning by imitating a process that takes billions of years?

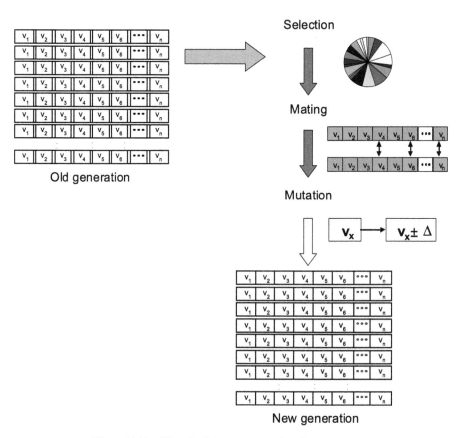

Figure 10.11. "Breeding" the next generation of chromosomes.

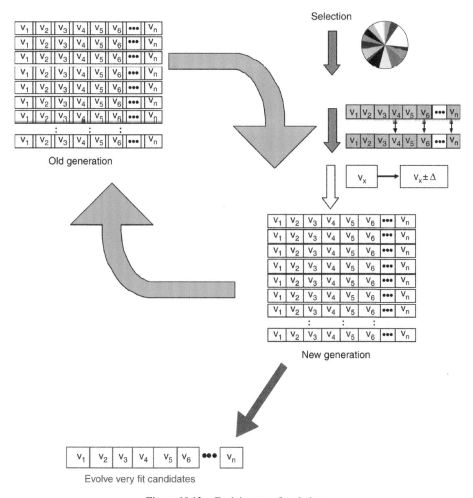

Figure 10.12. Evolving very fit solutions.

It must be appreciated that though evolutionary changes in large and very complex organisms do indeed take place over very long time spans, such organisms are comprised of incredibly large quantities of genetic building blocks, possess immensely complex functionalities, and have a vast number of (often interacting and sometimes contradictory) environmental adaptations that factor into the "objective functions" which need to be optimized for their continued survival. Simpler organisms, e.g. fruit flies, yield much faster evolutionary changes, and so can be used in biological experiments that are amenable to scientists' career schedules; and yet these "simpler" organisms are far more complex than the structure of most problems we encounter in industry. By comparison, typical industrial problems involve a mere handful of variables to be optimized, with the result that the ability of GA to handle non-monotonicities and discontinuities in the objective functions with aplomb makes the solution of such problems very viable. The time-limiting step usually is the evaluation of the fitness of members of the population should the objective function be computationally complex.

10.8. DISCOVERING PROFITABLE OPERATING STRATEGIES

Unleashing the power of genetic algorithms by their exploring multi-dimensional operating spaces enables the discovery of potentially profitable "sweet spots". For this pursuit of operating profitability, genetic algorithms are coupled with neural net (NN) models that correlate operating conditions with performance, thereby providing the objective functions for the GA to optimize. The neural net models are initally trained on historical operations. Their input parameters coincide with the variables (genes) of which the genetic algorithms' chromosomes are comprised. Their output represents the operational performance to be maximized, constituting feedback to the GA as a measure of chromosome fitness (Figure 10.13).

10.9. PRODUCT FORMULATION

Coupling GA–NN in this manner also yields powerful tools for discovering formulations for novel, high performing products. The neural nets deployed in

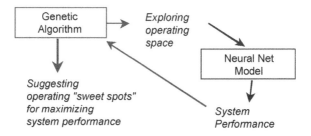

Figure 10.13. Discovering profitable operating strategies.

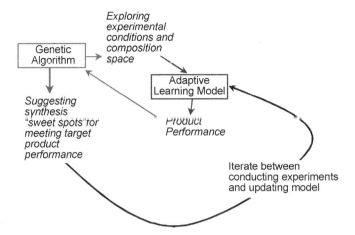

Figure 10.14. Discovering novel product formulations.

these couplings consist of performance models correlating compositional building blocks and synthesis conditions with the performance of the resulting product compounds. Most critical to success is the succinct characterization[47] of the synthesis conditions, reactant building blocks, and product performance prescribed by the input and output parameters used in constructing the performance model.

The genetic algorithm searches the experimental and composition space and provides conditions to the performance model, which then predicts the product performance (or structure) and feeds that back to the GA. This iterative process continues until systhesis conditions favoring the formation of products with desired characteristics are discovered. The performance model is being exercised in extrapolative mode in regions where actual data do not exist, hence its results are speculative. After all, the synthesis conditions of greatest interest are those which have not yet been actually encountered, or else the desired formulation would have already been synthesized! This approach is intended to identify new and potentially high yielding synthesis conditions which need to be experimentally validated. The suggestions for synthesis obtained from the GA form the basis on which the next set of experiments are conducted, the results of which are used to update the neural net performance model (Figure 10.14). Neural net models lend themselves to this type of repeated updating on account of their adaptive learning facility.

---

[47]While capturing all essential features.

The value added by this approach is its cost-effectiveness by very rapidly identifying promising synthesis conditions, thereby expediting the product formulation process.

REFERENCES

[1] Holland, J.H. (1975) *Adaptation in Natural and Artificial Systems*, The University of Michigan Press, Ann Arbor, MI.
[2] Holland, J.H. (1992) *Adaptation in Natural and Artificial Systems*, MIT Press, Cambridge, MA.
[3] Goldberg, D.E. (1989) *Genetic Algorithms in Search, Optimization and Machine Learning*, Addison-Wesley, Reading, MA.

Part III
Case Studies

Chapter 11

Harnessing the Technology for Profitability

The proof of the pudding is in the eating. However intriguing a technology may be, what sells in industry are solutions, not technology. This chapter is a prelude to the case studies that follow by way of outlining general modes of application, many of which are already in use.

11.1. PROCESS INDUSTRY APPLICATION MODES

11.1.1 Plant / Unit Monitoring and Performance Prediction

Adaptive learning models that capture the operating behavior of process plants and units are very rapidly constructed by extracting underlying patterns from historical plant data. The phenomena governing process unit behavior are very complex, involving complicated unit-specific hydrodynamics, chemical reactions and catalyst-specific kinetics, thermodynamic and physical properties associated with the wide variety of feeds usually encountered in plant operations, etc. Conventional models and simulations are not only expensive and time-consuming to develop, but they are also not easy to modify quickly and cost-effectively when dealing with configuration and operational changes. By contrast, neural net-based adaptive learning models are very rapidly developed if adequate plant operating data are available, and can be used to predict performance robustly when engineering judgment and experience are used in constraining their behavior appropriately.

Neural nets are able to predict conversion and selectivity when trained on historical data comprising of operating conditions, e.g. flow rates, treat rates, temperatures, pressures, and easily obtained properties characterizing the feed, such as density, cut points, aniline point, sulfur and nitrogen content, etc. (see Figure 11.1).

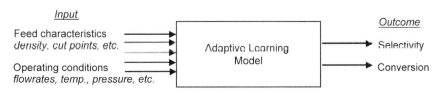

Figure 11.1. Process models predicting conversion and selectivity.

Of particular interest and use is that inversions of such models are as easily constructed as direct models, so that the models can indicate how units should be run in order to result in, for example, a desired conversion level when running a particular type of feed (see Figure 11.2). This is especially important for profitability planning in order to use relatively inexpensive but somewhat problematic feeds. Of course, it is essential that the problem be well posed. In other words, the model's inputs must be judiciously chosen so that they uniquely and completely govern the operating conditions (i.e. model outputs) that they are expected to correlate to.

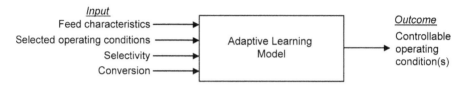

Figure 11.2. "Inverted" process models.

Conventional models and simulations cannot readily be so inverted due to the non-linear nature of the underlying governing equations.

11.1.2 Plant Environmental Emission
Plant emissions are also modeled very effectively in this manner, as shown in Figure 11.3.

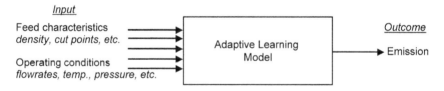

Figure 11.3. Plant environmental emission models.

11.1.3 In Situ Modeling Through Adaptive Learning
In order to capture the effects of start-up idiosyncrasies, catalyst activity uncertainties, upsets, and other unplanned events that occur during the course of any petroleum or chemical plant run, models initially trained on historical data can be deployed in situ so that they are continuously updated as fresh data become available as in Figure 11.4.

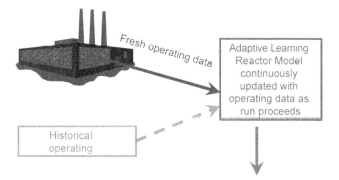

Figure 11.4. Model initially trained on historical data—and then continuously updated as fresh data become available.

11.1.4   Feed Translation / Property Characterization

Easily obtained properties can be mapped into valuable-to-know properties that are time-consuming, difficult and/or expensive to obtain. For example, the following crude properties are relatively easily obtained: API gravity, cut points, aniline point, refractive index, sulfur and nitrogen content. Their detailed chemical composition, e.g. high-performance liquid chromatography (HPLC) characteristics, is not as easily available (see Figure 11.5).

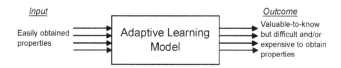

Figure 11.5.   Feed translation/property characterization models.

11.1.5   Product Quality Prediction

The quality and properties characterizing a chemical product can be correlated to the feed and other operating conditions for complex polymerization and other processes as shown in Figure 11.6.

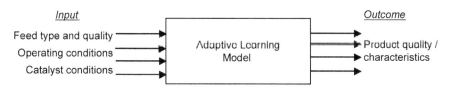

Figure 11.6.   Product quality prediction models.

11.1.6   Pilot Plant Analysis

Self-organizing systems are very effectively utilized in recognizing similarities and differences between pilot plant test runs, and identifying outliers and anomalous behavior when they occur (see Figure 11.7).

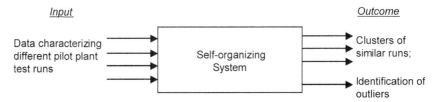

Figure 11.7.   Self-organizing systems analyze pilot plant behavior.

11.1.7   "Breeding" Fit Solutions

Coupling genetic algorithms (GAs) with data-driven adaptive learning models facilitates discovery of optimal operating strategies or novel, high performing formulations. Adaptive learning models are initially trained to correlate operating parameters or product composition with performance. Genetic algorithms then explore the operating or composition space and, with the help of the performance correlation models, discover potential "sweet spots" in this space for optimal solutions. In the case of product formulation, a very large number of experiments would be required to cover the entire formulation space. The approach suggested here significantly enhances the effectiveness of the experimental program by identifying those regions in the composition space which hold the greatest promise, and increases the probability of success (see Figure 11.8) by guiding the design of future experiments.

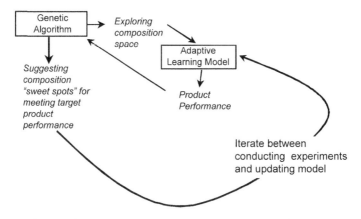

Figure 11.8.   GA coupled with adaptive models provide "fit" solutions.

11.2. BUSINESS APPLICATIONS

11.2.1 Marketing

Adaptive learning models can be constructed to capture customer behavior and preferences by correlating characteristics that constitute the customers' profiles with their observed behavior (see Figure 11.9).

Furthermore, a very large number of customers can be self-organized into clusters of those sharing similar characteristics (see Figure 11.10).

As this auto-clustering is performed without any intervening prejudgment of customer attributes, it is effective in objectively grouping customer according to their similarities. New potential customers can very rapidly be identified in terms of their anticipated behavior and preferences by quantitatively determining their proximity to clusters of known customers.

Figure 11.9.   Models predicting customer behavior.

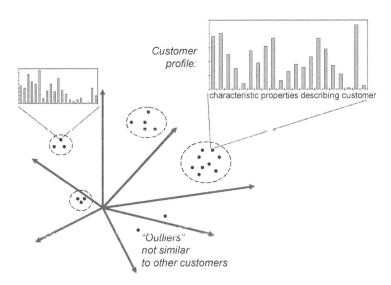

Figure 11.10.   Self-organizing customers into clusters with similar characteristics.

11.2.2 Credit Risk Prediction

In a manner similar to that outlined above, models can be constructed (see Figure 11.11) to predict potential applicants' credit risks by learning from historical data of proven credit worthiness (or the lack of it!). One form of output from such models would be the interval [0,1]. Data used for training the models would indicate an output of 0 for a bad credit outcome, and 1 for a good one. In the predictive mode an intermediate band, based on validation analysis, could be reserved for cases in which human intervention is called for. A large and varied historical training database together with a robust model would minimize the amount of required human intervention.

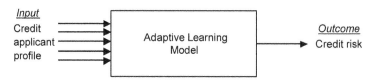

Figure 11.11.   Models predicting credit risk.

11.2.3   Detecting Biases in Demographic Data

It is often difficult to determine the existence of biases within demographic data because of the confounding influence of a large number of interrelated factors. One approach to solving this problem is to train neural net models that are kept blind to the investigated characteristic, to correlate other demographic characteristics with the measure of value, and then compare what the models have learned with the actual values for the individuals. For example, if salary-related gender discrimination is to be investigated (as illustrated in one of the case studies that follow), then gender-blind models are trained to correlate other characteristics such as experience, job description, levels of responsibility and education, etc., with salaries; and then look for systematic differences between the salaries prescribed by the models and actual salaries for the different genders. This approach isolates the effects of gender from factors that would otherwise confound the issue.

11.2.4   Assessing Business Environments

The suitability of a new location or environment can be assessed through models built on historical data on established business operations in different locations or environments. Data-driven adaptive learning models can digest a wide range of data such as demographics, economics, climate, different vendors, types of contracts, job conditions, etc. (see Figure 11.12).

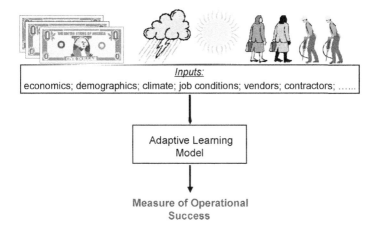

Figure 11.12. Models assessing new business locations/environments.

11.2.5 Competitive Intelligence

Thousands of documents can be computationally "read" very rapidly and a fingerprint generated for each one that captures the document's essential features. These documents could be patents, articles in the technical or business literature, news items or bulletins, etc. Similar documents can then be auto-classified into distinct clusters; each cluster representing the focal contents of its member documents.

Fingerprinting enables a document to be represented graphically, permitting almost instantaneous visual assimilation of its contents. Fingerprinting and auto-clustering can also capture the activity profiles of authors and competitors' inventors. As in forensic fingerprint matching, the activity profiles of authors, inventors or even companies in specific technical or business areas can rapidly be screened to identify key "players". The fingerprint of a cluster representing a specific technology can be used as a template to identify competitors' activities in that area.

This approach enables organizations to digest enormous amounts of information rapidly and efficiently. Furthermore, when implemented on-line it is able to scan current news and literature items and alert management on changes in markets and competitors' strategies. It is significant to point out that such competitive insight is developed entirely from data available in the public domain. It could significantly impact the way in which businesses keep their competitive edge.

11.3. CASE STUDIES THAT FOLLOW

The application of pattern recognition technology to enhance the profitability of industrial operations is limited only by the imagination. The following chapters in this section will attempt to stimulate such imagination through case study vignettes in a few selected areas in which the author has successfully implemented this approach. These case studies have been chosen both for their range of application as well as for the variety of techniques employed in their solution.

Chapter 12
Reactor Modeling Through In Situ Adaptive Learning [1]

12.1. BACKGROUND

Start-up idiosyncrasies, catalyst activity uncertainties, upsets, and other unplanned events that occur during the course of any petroleum or chemical plant run are the bane of plant engineers and managers. These unintended yet persistently occurring run anomalies make it difficult to predict the remaining course of the run as changing conditions considerably reduce the confidence one can place in pre-existing models. However, these difficulties can be alleviated by dynamically modeling reactor behavior "on the fly" during each run using an adaptive learning system. Such a system continually updates reactor models comprised of neural nets initially trained on historical plant data. The extrapolative capability of these models is enhanced by embedding constraints within them based on engineering judgment and operating experience. Constraining neural nets in this manner is essential for most industrial applications. This case study deals with predicting catalyst deactivation in a hydroprocessing reactor.

12.2. REACTOR CATALYST DEACTIVATION

A hydroprocessing reactor is one in which hydrogen is added to the feed in the presence of a catalyst and then heated in order to obtain a desirable product. One of the main goals is to decrease the level of sulfur in the product. The catalyst in the reactor deactivates with time during this process. This deactivation is influenced by many factors, making its mechanistic determination extremely difficult. Catalyst deactivation necessitates continuous increase of the reactor temperature to maintain product quality. This ultimately leads to ending the run and unit shutdown. It is important to be able to predict the end-of-run as the turnaround of a particular reactor unit impacts other units in the plant, and therefore has to be planned for with considerable deliberation. Furthermore, should it become necessary to extend the run, significant economic benefits are realized if the run extension were to be accomplished without undue product giveaway. There is, therefore, much to be gained by modelling the catalyst deactivation behavior within a reactor unit "on the fly" as the run proceeds in order to capture the idiosyncratic effects resulting from the start-up, upsets, use of different catalysts, etc.

12.3.   MODEL CONFIGURATION

A logically linear view of setting up a model of the reactor process would suggest that the model's inputs should be the feed characteristics and the reactor operating conditions, and the model outputs would be the product quality (i.e. sulfur content). However, as we are interested in the condition leading to the end-of-run (i.e. the reactor temperature), we wish to construct a model whose output is the reactor temperature and whose inputs are reactor operating conditions, feed characteristics, and product sulfur level. It is worth noting that a conventional mechanistic formulation (a very difficult and expensive procedure) would restrict the model's flow path to follow that of the reactor. In other words, the inputs and output to and from a conventional model would correspond to the inputs and output of the reactor. An inversion of a mechanistically derived model, enabling the operating temperature to be directly predicted for a specified product quality, would not be possible. The operating temperature for a specified product quality would have to be determined through trial-and-error iterations of such a model.

For our case a neural net model was constructed that directly predicted the reactor temperature required to attain the desired product quality. This model was configured as shown in Figure 12.1. The model predicted the reactor operating temperature using the following input variables describing the reactor feed characteristics and operating conditions.

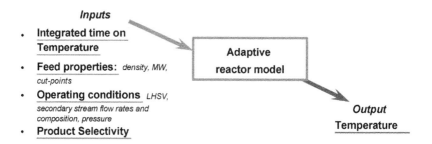

Figure 12.1.   Model configuration.

Feed characteristics:

- API gravity (i.e. feed density);
- sulfur wt in feed %;
- feed molecular weight;
- 50 and 90% cut points.

Operating conditions:

- feed rate (or LHSV);
- treat gas rate and purity;
- reactor pressure;
- days into run;
- product sulfur wt%.

As mentioned earlier, the output from the model was the reactor temperature.

Most importantly, to ensure robust model prediction, constraints were embedded into the model's architecture based on engineering judgment and plant operating experience. These constraints took the form of imposing monotonic behavior between certain input parameters and the dependent output.

12.4.   IN SITU MODELING SCHEME

The overall modeling scheme comprised of training neural net models on historical data from several runs. The models are subsequently updated adaptively as fresh data from new runs become available (Figure 12.2), thereby capturing the idiosyncratic effects resulting from the start-up, upsets, use of different catalysts, etc., as the run proceeds.

The extent to which such models are permitted to adapt to fresh data is a critical factor in their predictive performance. If the training level for updates is too intensive, then the historical training through which the models learned the nuances of how different feeds and operating conditions affected the reactor behavior would be "forgotten". On the other hand, an insufficient level of update learning would not enable the models to capture adequately the catalyst deactivation of the fresh run. This tuning issue was addressed during the model validation process and is described in the next section. The models were trained on historical data from certain runs, and

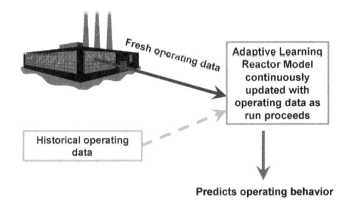

Figure 12.2. Model initially trained on historical data—and subsequently continuously updated as fresh data become available.

then updated in a mock in situ mode point by point using historical data for other runs.

The final deployment of such a system best takes the form of several adaptive learning reactor models (ALRM) in parallel as shown in Figure 12.3. These models are updated with a varying degree of mix between fresh data and historical data while the new run is underway. Such an approach enables flexibility in weighting the fresh data against historical experience, and is of particular value if

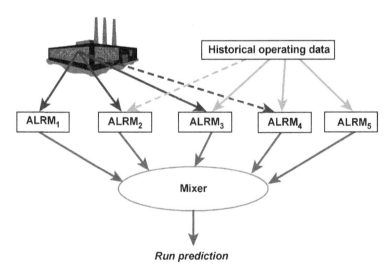

Figure 12.3. Multiple model deployment.

the type of feed encountered in the new run were to change abruptly and significantly. In that case historical data would be searched for feeds similar to the newly encountered ones, and the possessive "memories" refreshed by training them on these recently identified historical data.

12.5. VALIDATION PROCEDURE

Prior to deploying such a system in the field, the following validation procedure is followed. Neural net models are trained on historical data from several previous runs. As mentioned earlier, these models should incorporate the engineering judgment and operating experience of domain experts by embedding constraints in their architectures. They are then validated on other historical runs not used in their initial training process. This validation process consists of the models being given data, one step at a time, from a hitherto "unseen" run, and then tested by being required to predict this run's behavior from that point in time to its end. The degree of intensity of the updating training is adjusted to yield optimal predictions of the remaining length of the unit's run, which is that part of the run as yet unseen by the model during the update-training process. The validation serves to select the best performing models as well as establish tuning factors for the extent of update learning.

12.6. VALIDATION RESULTS

A neural net model was trained on historical data from two runs. It was then tested in a mock in situ mode on a different run by updating it one data point at a time. The interval between each new data point was approximately 1 week. The net was trained only on the data up to each successive weekly update; the temperature data for the rest of the run were withheld from the model. However, as the data for the entire length of the run were available in the historical record, after each "weekly" update the net was given the operating history and feed characteristics for the rest of the run and was required to predict the reactor temperature until the run's end. Figure 12.4 shows the net's prediction prior to any update on the "new" run. This is the prediction results for the new run based only on the initial training derived from two prior different runs.

The ordinate (*y*-axis) shows the reactor temperature; and each tick on the abscissa represents a time interval of approximately 1 week. Though these results show that the model has learned the effects of changing feeds and operating

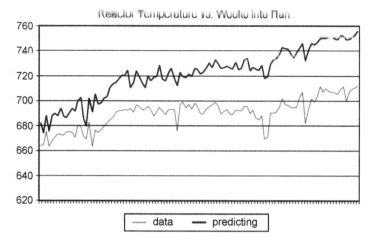

Figure 12.4.   Model predictions based only on prior runs.

conditions on the reactor temperature rather well as indicated by the predicted "wiggles" qualitatively following the actual temperature "wiggles", the model is unable to predict the catalyst deactivation behavior (i.e. the overall temperature trend) correctly.

After updating the model by training it on the first five data points of the new run, it is able to predict the rest of that run remarkably well (Figure 12.5). In this figure, the thick blue line represents the updated training, the red line is

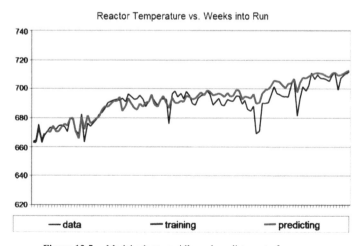

Figure 12.5.   Model adapts rapidly and predicts rest of new run.

the model prediction, and the thin dark blue line indicates the actual temperature data.

12.7. ROLES PLAYED BY MODELING AND PLANT OPERATIONAL TEAMS

The plant staff and the model developers scope the project and jointly decide on the specificity and quantity of historical data necessary for a successful project. The on-site staff gathers and transfers the required historical data to the developers, who then build prototype models. The evolution from prototype to deployable models takes place in a joint effort between the two teams through the validation process. Domain expertise for the model development is obtained from the combined team, with the plant staff providing process insight gleaned from their experience with the unit, and the modelers providing modeling expertise and execution as well as any process expertise they may have acquired though other similar modeling experiences.

A vital element in ensuring success is that the plant staff assume ownership of the models as they are developed and become fully involved in putting them through their paces. This is usually a very exciting phase of the project as the team gels together in discovering what the models are saying and why.

Field deployment of the modeling system is largely dictated by the plant's needs and work processes. It is important that the modeling team provide continuing support for the system, and help train operators in its use.

12.8. COMPETITIVE ADVANTAGE DERIVED THROUGH THIS APPROACH

A major limitation of conventional approaches to estimating catalyst deactivation is that a run has to be well underway before its particular catalyst deactivation characteristics can be ascertained; and even then uncertainties arise if the run is subject to upsets. The advantages of the in situ adaptive learning system are:

- being able to predict unit behavior very early into the run
- stretching the units for higher profitability by
  - enabling the use of new (higher activity) catalyst
  - changing feed cut point with minimum giveaway
  - extending run-length with minimum giveaway

- coping with future operating changes
  - ○ enabling the use of different feeds
  - ○ extending the range of processing conditions
- handling upsets

REFERENCE

[1] Bhagat, P.M. & Ellis, E.S. (2000) *In-Situ Learning while Refining: Reaction Engineering in the 21st Century*, North American Symposium on Chemical Reaction Engineering (NASCRE 1), Houston, January 2000.

Chapter 13

Predicting Plant Stack Emissions to Meet Environmental Limits

13.1. BACKGROUND

A refinery with a reactor unit much larger than standard units of its type was required to meet stack emission specifications. What makes this case especially interesting is that the allowed limits for the particulate emissions were on an absolute mass rate basis rather than a percentage of the stack gases; and the specification was based on that for a unit of average size, thereby making it a very challenging target for a very large reactor to meet. In order to optimize operational profits, it was essential to be able to use low cost feeds with high sulfur content without exceeding the stack emissions regulatory limits.

The goal was to model the unit's behavior in order to be able to predict the stack emissions given the feed to the unit and the operating conditions, and then to identify operating windows which would permit the profitable use of high sulfur content feeds without exceeding the limits for stack emissions.

13.2. REACTOR FLOW AND MODEL CONFIGURATION

A simplified overall flow diagram for the reactor unit is shown in Figure 13.1. The feed and a regeneration stream flow into the primary reactor. The effluents from the reactor go through off-gas boilers and scrubbers before entering the exhaust stacks. Domain experts identified potentially important input parameters that governed the unit's behavior. This list of parameters was screened for mathematical resonance with the intended outcome (the rate of particulates emitted in the stack) and was subsequently pruned to generate the following set of key variables used as inputs for the final model:

- feed rate;
- feed sulfur content;
- regeneration stream flow-rate;
- air flow-rate to gas boilers;
- purge stream flow-rate;
- catalyst circulation rate.

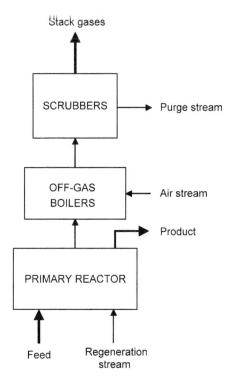

Figure 13.1.   Simplified reactor flow schematic.

The resulting model was sufficiently accurate and dependable so as not to require detailed feed characterization except for the sulfur content in the feed. As always, the aim is to develop a robust model as simply as possible and with the fewest number of independent variables; ensuring, however, that all the parameters critical to the unit's behavior are accounted for. The model configuration is illustrated in Figure 13.2.

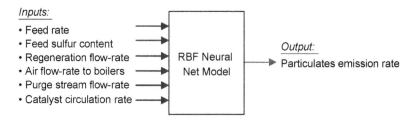

Figure 13.2.   Model configuration.

A radial basis function (RBF) neural net architecture was used here as it performed two functions simultaneously: (i) predicting the stack emissions and (ii) indicating the proximity of the predicted case(s) to the conditions over which the net was trained, thereby serving as an index of confidence to be placed in the prediction(s). The latter capability was essential given the grave consequences, both environmentally and financially, if the unit were not to meet the specified regulatory limits.

13.3. MODEL TRAINING AND RESULTS

Data for 92 distinctly different historical operating conditions were available for training the neural net model. The Jack-knifing cross-validation method described in an earlier chapter was used in order not to "over-fit" any noise in the data. The 92 data points were randomly distributed into four buckets of 23 points each. From these four buckets, four sets of data were assembled to train and validate RBF nets. A different bucket was earmarked for validation in each set, while the remaining three buckets were used for training in that set. Hence, each net was trained on 69 data points and validated by predicting 23 data points. Different RBF nets (having different numbers of hidden nodes and using different randomizing seeds for initial distribution of the nodes within the data space) were so trained.

The final net structure was chosen on the basis of the minimum prediction errors, and that was then trained on all the data to produce the final model. Figure 13.3 shows the net's predictions as a parity plot against the measured

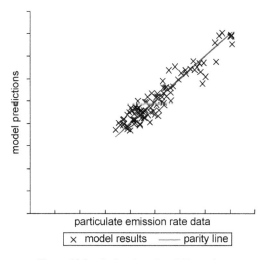

Figure 13.3. Parity plot of model's results.

emission rates. The final model exhibited a coefficient of determination, r^2, of 0.89[48] which is very good given the scatter in the data.

13.4.   IDENTIFYING OPTIMAL OPERATING WINDOWS FOR ENHANCING PROFITS

The neural net model was used to discover the effects of varying operating conditions on the stack particulates emissions rate when using feeds of differing sulfur content. Operational procedures dictated certain ratios between various operating conditions which were not to be violated, and those constraints were adhered to while exercising the model. Exploring the non-linear behavior of the reactor led to identifying optimal operating envelopes for feeds with high sulfur content, within which particulates emission was confined to the regulatory limits.

The model's findings confirmed the expected general trends of increasing emissions with increasing feed sulfur content and increasing regeneration flow-rate. However, non-linear and complex interactions between the input parameters and outcomes resulted in interesting and unanticipated results, such as the effects of varying purge rates on the stack emissions, giving the opportunity for identifying operating parameter envelopes within which optimal operating strategies could be developed for running high sulfur feeds, thereby maximizing operating profitability. Additionally, the model provided a means for predicting the consequences for contemplated operational changes.

---

[48]An r^2 of 1 indicates a perfect fit; an r^2 of 0 results from a model which merely predicts the average outcome for all cases. A negative r^2 indicates that the model is anti-correlated with the data.

Chapter 14
Predicting Fouling / Coking in Fired Heaters

14.1. BACKGROUND

In essence a petroleum refinery or chemical plant may be thought of as a series of tubes through which feedstock is converted to more valuable products through chemical reactions and by adding and removing heat and different material components at various points along the tubes. Hydrocarbons constitute the bulk of the material flowing through these tubes. As the flowing material is heated, coke is formed and, along with other foulants, is deposited inside the tubes. This phenomenon is prevalent in the tubes of fired heaters and heat exchangers. Fired heater tubes are most vulnerable to the formation and deposition of coke as certain sections of the tubes experience very high heat flux and consequently high temperatures. As the coke layer builds up with time, the heat transfer resistance of the composite tube wall and coke layer increases, thereby requiring increasing skin, or tube metal, temperature (TMT) in order to maintain the amount of heat transferred to the flowing fluid. Ultimately, the tube metal temperature reaches the pipe's metallurgical limit and the unit has to be shut down and decoked. Unplanned unit shutdown can be prevented by predicting coke or foulant deposition rates and consequent TMT increase. This enables the plant operator to develop coordinated operating strategies and make operating decisions for maximizing asset utilization.

This case study deals with a fired pipestill heater that experienced high local TMT increases in one of its tubes. This resulted in shorter run lengths, as the heater tubes needed frequent decoking in that particular section. It was not clear what exactly caused this unusually high coking rate, whether it was related to running heavier crudes or some other operating factor(s). Premature shutdowns being very costly, a predictive tool was commissioned that would allow improved planning for shutdowns, and for determining how to make changes in operating conditions to increase run length.

14.2. MODEL CONFIGURATION

The model needed to account for complex interactions among many variables such as varying feeds and operating conditions. For instance, higher feed rates require

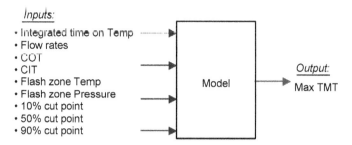

Figure 14.1. Model configuration.

higher heat flux which increases the coking propensity; at the same time higher flow velocities could shear off some of the deposited coke. A back-propagation neural net model was constructed to predict the TMT at the most severe location in the tubes. The model used the following key operating parameters and feed characteristics as inputs (see Figure 14.1):

- integrated time on temperature (temperature–time history);
- flow rates;
- coil outlet temperature (COT);
- coil inlet temperature (CIT);
- flash zone temperature and pressure;
- 10, 50, and 90% feed cut points.

Historical data for two runs (representing two and a half years of operation) were used to train the net. Engineering judgment and knowledge gained from operating experience were embedded in the model in the form of monotonic constraints between individual input parameters and the dependent outcome (TMT at the most severe location), enabling robust extrapolation. The trained net learned to extract patterns from historical data, building an internal model to account for coke lay-down. It correlated the unit's temperature–time history, feed characteristics, and operating conditions with the tube metal temperatures.

Integrated time on temperature accounted for the temperature history seen by the furnace from the start of run up to the instant for each datum. Eq. (14.1) defines this variable:

$$\text{Time\_on\_Temperature} = \int_{t=\text{start-of-run}}^{t=\text{present}} (\text{TMT}) dt \qquad (14.1)$$

Several neural net models with different degrees of freedom[49] were trained on historical data for two runs (representing two and a half years of operation) and

---

[49] i.e. different number of hidden nodes.

then used to predict the critical TMT for a different (third) run. The final model was the one best able to predict the TMT for the third run. The results from this model are described in the next section.

14.3. MODEL RESULTS

Figures 14.2 and 14.3 show how well the model learned to correlate the critical TMT with the operating conditions and feeds used in runs #1 and #2.

Figure 14.4 shows the model's predictions of TMT for run #3 which not used for training it.

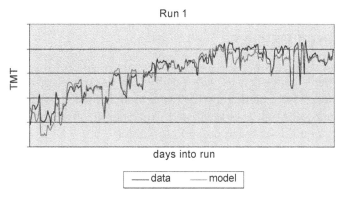

Figure 14.2. Model training results for run #1.

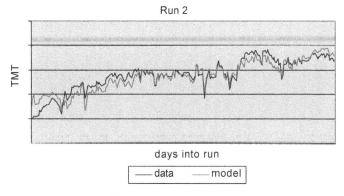

Figure 14.3. Model training results for run #2.

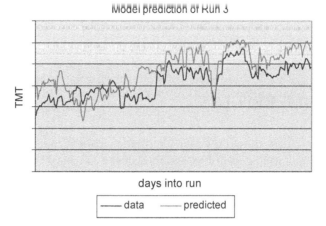

Figure 14.4. Model predictions for run #3.

14.4. CONCLUSIONS

Post-deployment feedback was very positive, as the model proved reliable and useful. By successfully predicting TMT, the model enabled prediction of end-of-run and planning for unit shutdown, and exploring the effects of changing feeds and operating conditions for improved profitability.

This modeling approach has proven successful in predicting coking/fouling in a wide range of fired and unfired heat transfer equipment. Neural net models can be updated continuously as fresh data become available, thereby accurately capturing nuances of a specific unit's behavior.

Chapter 15
Predicting Operational Credits

15.1. BACKGROUND

This case deals with a refinery unit that included a number of reactors in parallel. The feed lines to these reactors did not have individual flow controls; hence there was maldistribution in the flow rates through them. This flow maldistribution was manifested in the form of a temperature maldistribution, resulting in additional reagent consumption in the reactors and poorer product quality control. The question to be answered was whether or not the process credits realized by correcting the flow maldistribution would justify the cost of installing the needed individual flow controllers.

The chemical reactions involved and the parallel reactors' hydrodynamics were too complicated for a cost effective and timely mechanistic modeling and simulation solution to be developed. Conventional statistical methods were unable to identify the effects of maldistribution on the reagent consumption from historical plant data.

15.2. ISSUES

Screening the historical plant data revealed significant noise in them. The filling of the reagent holding tanks was performed manually at the operators' discretion, resulting in considerable uncertainty as to the actual amount of reagent consumed at any given time. The neural net model developed to correlate the reagent consumption with the temperature maldistribution and other key process operating conditions was able to surmount the difficulties posed by the noise in the data. Fitting noise in the data was prevented by embedding constraints in the net while it was learning to extract patterns from the data in the process of developing its internal model. These constraints were based on rules derived from an operating understanding of the process and, in addition to avoid fitting noise, they helped the net to develop a model which extrapolated robustly. The concept of embedding constraints in order to incorporate available knowledge into an empirically based training process has been described in previous chapters.

15.3. MODEL CONFIGURATION

The configuration of the neural net adaptive learning model is shown in Figure 15.1. Inputs to the model included key operating conditions and the temperature maldistribution. The dependent outcome predicted by the model was the rate of reagent consumption. The temperature maldistribution was represented by a measure of the deviation from uniformity as expressed in Eq. (15.1)

$$\text{Temp\_maldistr} = \sqrt{\frac{\sum_{i=1}^{N}(T_i - T_{\text{avg}})^2}{N}} \tag{15.1}$$

where

$$T_{\text{avg}} = \frac{\sum_{i=1}^{N} T_i}{N}$$

and N is the number of reactors in parallel.

Several neural net models with different architectures and degrees of constraints were trained on the data to ensure consistency in the extracted patterns and trends. This was affirmed by verifying that the various models behaved similarly. Embedded constraints in the model enforced monotonic relationships, between

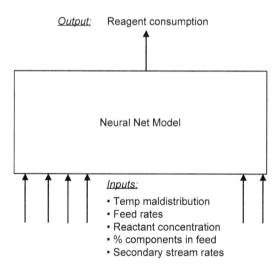

Figure 15.1. Model configuration.

the individual inputs and the dependent outcome, which process experts specified based on their experience with plant operations.

15.4. MODEL RESULTS

Once the models were trained on the data and it was determined that their results agreed with one another, they were used to determine the credits that would be realized by correcting the maldistribution. This was accomplished by exercising the models to yield predictions for the reagent consumption at different levels of temperature maldistribution while keeping all the other operating conditions constant at levels representing their average values over approximately 2 years of plant operation. These results are shown in Figure 15.2 in which the solid line represents the models' prediction of the reagent consumption (in units/day) in excess of the consumption level predicted under conditions of zero maldistribution.

The average maldistribution observed over the 2 years of operation was determined to be 2.5°. For this degree of maldistribution the model predicted additional consumption of 55 units/day over the level corresponding to uniform flow distribution. This anticipated saving in reagent consumption by correcting flow maldistribution justified the cost associated with installing the flow monitors and controllers with a payback period of less than a year.

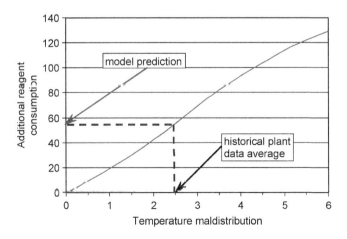

Figure 15.2. Models predicting additional consumption due to maldistribution.

15.5. PLANT FOLLOW-UP

The plant installed the flow monitors and controller on the basis of this analysis. A year after the flow maldistribution was corrected, the plant reported an average reduction in the reagent consumption of 55 units/day!

That the results were exactly as predicted is somewhat fortuitous. The significant point of this case study is that conventional approaches were unable to solve this problem, and the plant would very likely not have invested in the modification were it not for the pattern recognition technology-based modeling analysis.

Chapter 16
Pilot Plant Scale-up by Interpreting Tracer Diagnostics[50]

16.1. BACKGROUND

A commercial-scale fluidized bed reactor was to be designed based on pilot plant experience. Experimenting with the pilot plant yielded operating conditions that resulted in very good performance. In order to scale up the pilot plant results, it was necessary to determine the flow regime associated with the successful operating conditions. In this case the multi-phase flow regime is characterized by the following five parameters:

- liquid and gas dispersion coefficients;
- liquid and gas (actual, rather than superficial) velocities;
- two-phase interfacial area.

A hydrodynamic model was constructed to simulate the flow process in the reactor. The inputs to this model included these five parameters, and the model would then predict the concentration profiles of a tracer, introduced at the reactor inlet, as functions of time and location along the length of the reactor. The flow regime would be established by those values of the five parameters that produced the closest fit between the model's tracer predictions and the experimental results of actual measurements made of the tracer concentrations.

16.2. ISSUE

The simulation model's formulation involved very complex non-linear differential equations. The model's non-linearity and complexity precluded the possibility of inverting it so that the tracer results could be fed in as inputs and the values of the flow parameters obtained as outputs. The only way to obtain the flow parameter values would have been by trial and error, and it is an understatement to say that that is not an attractive option!

---

[50]Collaboration with R.M. Koros and P.R. Ponzi.

16.3. GENETIC ALGORITHM–SIMULATION MODEL COUPLING

This problem of determining the values of the flow regime parameters was solved by coupling a genetic algorithm (GA) to the reactor simulation model. The genetic algorithm searched within the parametric space and found the values of the parameters that gave the best fit between the simulation model and the measured tracer data.

Figure 16.1 is a schematic diagram of the reactor. Figure 16.2 is a schematic illustrating the tracer flow through the reactor. Figure 16.3 shows an actual set of tracer measurements along the reactor length following an injected tracer pulse upstream of the reactor. Simulated tracer results from the model are shown in Figure 16.4. The configuration in which the genetic algorithm was coupled to the simulation model is schematically illustrated in Figure 16.5.

To summarize, let us step through what this GA–simulation model coupling is intended to accomplish and how it does so.

- The aim is to determine those values of the hydrodynamic parameters that enable the model to produce tracer concentration profiles (as functions of

Figure 16.1.   Reactor schematic.

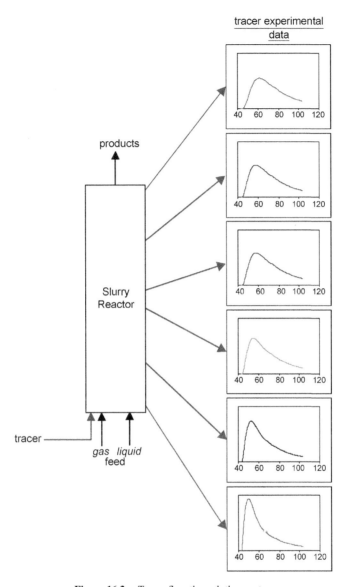

Figure 16.2.   Tracer flow through the reactor.

time) at various points along the reactor's length that most closely fit the actually measured tracer profiles. The model computes the simulated tracer behavior at each point in the reactor where actual tracer measurements were made. The five hydrodynamic parameters are: gas and liquid dispersion

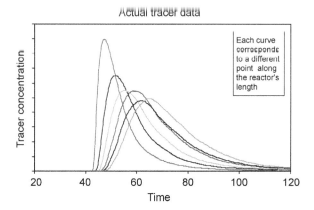

Figure 16.3.   Actual tracer measurements—concentration vs. time.

coefficients; actual (rather than superficial) gas and liquid velocities; and the gas–liquid interface area.

- The GA explores the five-dimensional space of the hydrodynamic parameters and suggests values to the model, which then computes the tracer profiles at various points along the reactor's length.
- For each suggested set of parameters, the model's tracer profiles are compared with the profiles measured during an actual run. This is done by calculating the sum of the mean squared differences between the model's result and the measured data for each point on each tracer curve. This sum represents the error between the model's result and the actual reactor operation, and the GA's task is to obtain a set of hydrodynamic parameter values that minimizes this error.

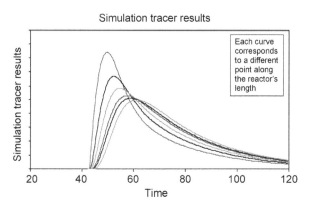

Figure 16.4.   Simulation tracer results—concentration vs. time.

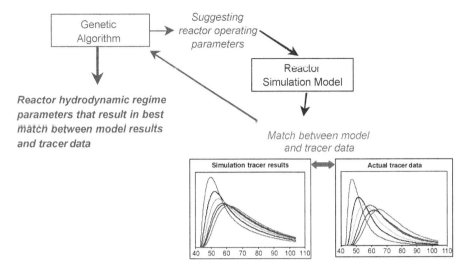

Figure 16.5.   Genetic algorithm–simulation model coupling.

16.4.   RESULTS AND CONCLUSION

The objective function to be maximized was the similarity between the measured and the simulated tracer curves. It was important to match (i) the shape of the curves and (ii) the inflection points in the curves indicating the times at which the tracer concentration peaked at each location.

A comparison between the simulation results and actual measurements at two of the six locations in the reactor is shown in Figure 16.6 after the genetic algorithm has found optimal values of the hydrodynamic parameters that give the best fit for the tracer curves at all locations within the reactor.

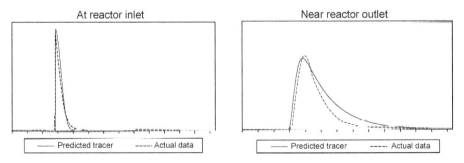

Figure 16.6.   Comparison between simulation predictions and actual measurements for flow parameter values giving the best fit.

Determining the values of the flow regime parameters for well-performing pilot plant operations enabled successful design of the reactor for the commercial plant. This approach can also be applied profitably for trouble-shooting existing plant operations. Ascertaining a plant's operating regime makes it possible to diagnose the cause of operational malfunctions.

Chapter 17

Predicting Distillation Tower Temperatures: Mining Data for Capturing Distinct Operational Variability

17.1. BACKGROUND

The quality of the product made in a distillation tower is governed by the temperatures in the series of trays within the tower. This case study deals with the development of a model for predicting temperatures in six distillation tower trays under varying operating conditions. The tray temperatures are important in that they determine the distillation tower's product quality.

17.2. ISSUE

The issue in this particular case was that operating data had been gathered on a minute-by-minute basis, resulting in 10,000 data points representing 1 week of operation. To avoid biasing training by a large number of data points over periods of operations where conditions essentially remained unchanged, the data needed to be mined for identifying distinctly different operating conditions within this dataset before they were used to develop a model for predicting the tower tray temperatures.

17.3. MODEL CONFIGURATION

The input parameters used as inputs to the model included the feed rate, feed temperature, flow rates and chemical composition of the reflux streams, purge flow rate, and the rate of steam flowing to the reboiler. The outcomes predicted by the model were the temperatures in six trays at different positions in the tower. The model configuration is shown in Figure 17.1.

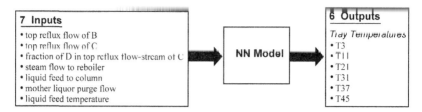

Figure 17.1.   Model configuration.

17.4.   IDENTIFYING DISTINCTLY DIFFERENT OPERATING CONDITIONS

The self-organizing methodology described in the earlier chapters was used to separate the data into clusters identifying distinctly different operating conditions. This procedure was performed on the seven-dimensional input data set. The data for each variable were first normalized over the 10,000 sets of data. The normalized value of each datum, n, for each variable, i, was obtained as in Eq. (17.1):

$$\hat{I}_{i,n} = \frac{(I_{i,n} - m_i)}{\sigma_i} \quad \text{where} \quad m_i = \frac{\sum_{n=1}^{N} I_{i,n}}{N}, \quad \sigma_i = \frac{\sqrt{\sum_{n=1}^{N} (I_{i,n} - m_i)^2}}{N-1}$$

(17.1)

and N is the total number of data points.

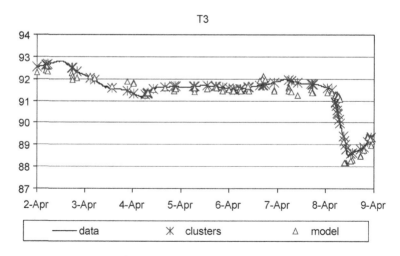

Figure 17.2.   Temperature for tray #3.

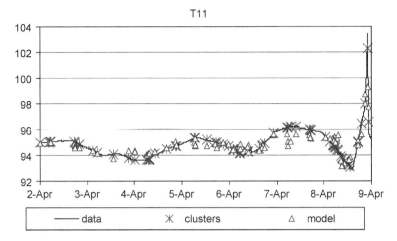

Figure 17.3. Temperature for tray #11.

Once so normalized, the *N* data points were self-organized into clusters containing similar conditions. Of the 10,000 points, 81 distinctly different clusters emerged. These 81 operating conditions were used to train the neural net model.

17.5. RESULTS

Figures 17.2–17.7 show the results of the model for each of the six tray temperature predictions. The solid line represents the actual temperature data,

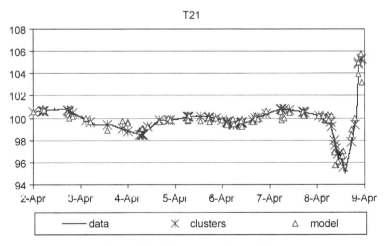

Figure 17.4. Temperature for tray #21.

Pattern Recognition in Industry

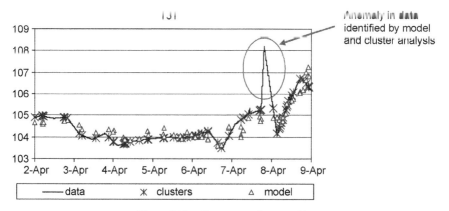

Figure 17.5. Temperature for tray #31.

the crosses indicate the data points represented by each of the 81 clusters, and the triangles show the results obtained from the model.

In addition to correlating the operating conditions to the tray temperatures successfully, the results of the model and the cluster analysis showed there to be an anomaly in the data for one of the days over a brief time interval (Figure 17.5). The excursion in the temperature data for tray #31 at approximately 8 p.m. on April 7

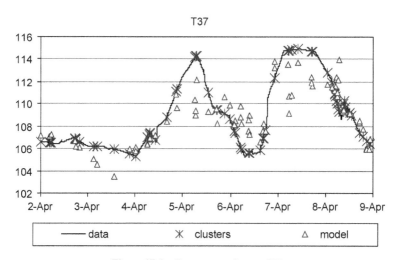

Figure 17.6. Temperature for tray #37.

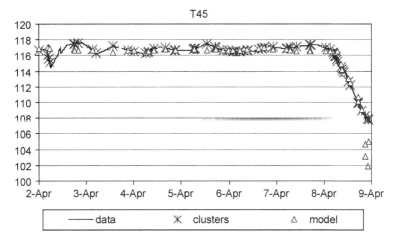

Figure 17.7. Temperature for tray #45.

did not correspond to operating conditions that were different in any way from those immediately preceding or following it. Subsequent examination of the data led to the conclusion that for that brief period the temperature recorded at that location was incorrect.

Chapter 18

Enabling New Process Design Based on Laboratory Data

18.1. BACKGROUND

This case involves manufacture of a polymer product to be used for the food industry. Consequently, stringent regulations had to be met, requiring the removal of residual monomers from the liquid polymer product. In this case, the use of a novel catalyst required designing a new back-end separation process for removing the undesired monomers.

Designing a system for removing a particular component from the liquid phase requires an understanding of the liquid–vapor equilibrium behavior of each component in the mixture. However, no fundamental thermodynamic models were available for determining the liquid–vapor properties (hereafter referred to as partition coefficients) of the three monomers to be removed from the liquid phase of the non-ideal mixture in this particular case. The partition coefficient for a component in a mixture is instrumental in determining its liquid–vapor phase equilibrium properties that govern the amount of that component present in the liquid phase. Therefore, determining the most suitable operating conditions for removing a component from the liquid mixture requires knowledge of the partition coefficients under a wide range of mixture conditions.

Partition coefficients of components in non-ideal mixtures are complex functions dependent on the temperature, pressure, and composition of the mixture. As no fundamental thermodynamic models were available for the system in this case, pattern recognition technology was harnessed to develop data-driven models from experimental laboratory results, thereby enabling the process designers to develop the commercial process. The models had to be robust as they would be required to extrapolate beyond laboratory conditions.

18.2. MODEL CONFIGURATION—BI-LEVEL FOCUS FOR "SPOT-LIGHTING" REGION OF INTEREST

Three models were built to predict thermodynamic partition coefficients for the three monomers in the mixture under various conditions. As the mixture was highly non-ideal, the partition coefficients were functions of temperature, pressure, and composition. Inputs to the models were:

- pressure
- temperature
- wt% polymer in mixture (i.e. the conversion)
- wt% monomers in the feed gas
- wt % monomers in the product
- molecular weight of the polymer

The outputs from the three models were the partition coefficients of each of the three monomers, respectively. As it was critical for these models to extrapolate robustly beyond the laboratory conditions on which they were trained, constraints to impose monotonic relationships between individual independent variables and the dependent outcomes were embedded into their architecture. The monotonic directions for each constraint were specified on the basis of known fundamental thermodynamic principles.

Preliminary model development indicated no issue with predicting partition functions for two of the three monomers for this application. The regulations were most stringent on the permissible amount of the third monomer in the product, and therefore high accuracy was required in predicting its partition function at very low levels. A single model covering the entire range of conditions for this monomer could not adequately deliver the desired accuracy at very low levels. Bi-level focus was provided by developing two separate models for this monomer: one covering the entire range of partition function values and the other focusing on the low end of the range through "spot-lighted" scaling. The latter model would not be as accurate at high values of the partition function but would afford the needed accuracy at the low end.

"Spot-lighted" scaling was accomplished by specifying values for the mean, maximum, and minimum values used in the equation[51] for preconditioning the output variable (partition function for monomer #3) data (Eq. 18.1)

$$O_{\text{Scaled}}(p) = \frac{1}{1 + e^{\left\{-(O(p) - \text{Mean}) \cdot \text{Limit} \cdot 2/(\text{Max} - \text{Min})\right\}}} \qquad (18.1)$$

for $p = [1, N]$ where N is the number of data available for training.

The value of Mean is chosen as the mid-point of the range to be spot-lighted; Max and Min are chosen at the high and low ends of this range.

All the models were cross-validated in the usual way.

---

[51] See section in earlier chapter dealing with preconditioning data for back-propagation neural nets.

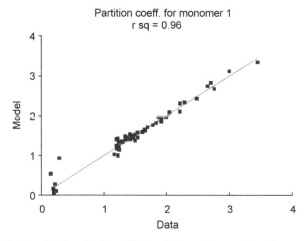

Figure 18.1.   Results of model for prediction of the partition coefficient for monomer #1.

18.3.   MODEL RESULTS

Figures 18.1 and 18.2 show parity plots for the final models built for predicting the partition functions for monomers #1 and #2. The abscissa represents the experimental data, the ordinate the model results.

Figures 18.3 and 18.4 show the results of both the models for predicting the partition coefficient for monomer #3 over the full range of values for the coefficient and the low end, respectively. The blue points represent the coarse grain

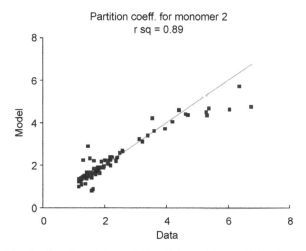

Figure 18.2.   Results of model for prediction of the partition coefficient for monomer #2.

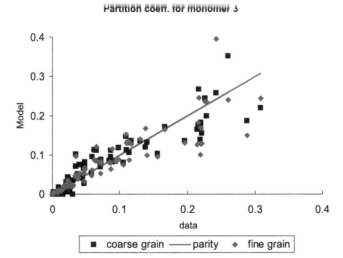

Figure 18.3.   Results of models for prediction of the partition coefficient for monomer #3 over the entire range
of values.

model; the red points indicate the fine grain model which "spot-lights" the low end
(which is more important from the design point of view).

Greater precision is needed at low values of partition coefficient for monomer #3
and so, as shown in Figure 18.5, the fine grain model (red points) is used if

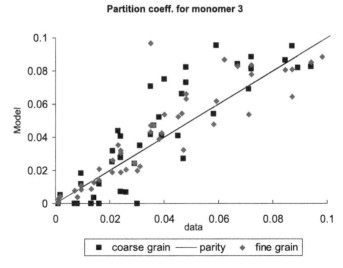

Figure 18.4.   Results of models for prediction of the partition coefficient for monomer #3 at the important
(i.e. low) values.

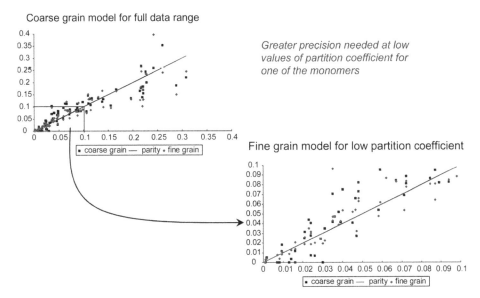

Figure 18.5. Bi-level focus for improved precision at low end.

the partition function is less than 0.1. The coarse grain model (blue points) is used if the partition function is greater than 0.1.

18.4.   CONCLUSION

Bi-level focusing to spot-light a critically important region and embedding constraints in the models for robust extrapolation worked well in achieving the goals for this application. Post-deployment feedback from the client was very positive. The models proved to be reliable and were very useful in the successful design of the polymer manufacturing process.

Chapter 19

Forecasting Price Changes of a Composite Basket of Commodities

19.1. BACKGROUND

Inevitably at cocktail parties practitioners of pattern recognition technology are asked, "Can you predict the stock market?" The response to this varies depending on the quantity and quality of the libations imbibed and the relationship between the questioner and the respondent! On a serious note, issues such as the concept of efficient markets, psychological factors, the time scales involved, etc., place a discussion of this topic outside the scope of this book. This chapter deals with forecasting based on potential cause-and-effect relationships in which leading indicator(s) drive the lagging factors of interest.

The development of a capital investment strategy required forecasting the change in advance of an index representing the transacted price of a basket of materials and manufactured equipment for a particular industry. This required identifying relevant leading indicators from public domain economic data, determining the corresponding lead time intervals between the identified indicators and the index, and then correlating changes in the indicators with future changes in the index.

19.2. APPROACH AND MODEL CONFIGURATION

The following information was available for forecasting the industry-specific index:

- historical general economic and price index data in great detail in the public domain
- forecasts of these by various economic forecasting organizations
- historical industry-specific transacted price information gathered by the industry-specific client

Hundreds of economic indices (time series) from the public domain were examined for their potential as candidate leading indicators. It is important to note that each time series was converted, where necessary, to reflect the *change* in

149

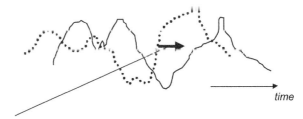

time

Slide leading indicator candidate forward, checking for
resonance with index of interest

Figure 19.1.   Identifying leading indicators by synchronizing the time series.

value over the previous quarter rather than the absolute value. Hence, in the
rest of this chapter when we refer to an index we are referring to the change of
its value.

Each candidate was automatically screened for suitability: the degree to which
each one's time series resonated with that of the index of interest was calculated
over a range of systematically varying lead-time intervals (from 5 to 20 quarters).
A "snippet"[52] of each candidate time series over a certain time interval was
compared with a snippet over a similar time interval of the index. These snippets
were slid over each other until the lead-time interval yielding the maximum
resonance was found (see Figure 19.1). This lead interval along with the extent of
resonance between the two snippets was then recorded as associated with each
candidate leading indicator. This process was repeated for different snippet lengths
ranging from 30 to 150 quarters. A snippet length of 40 quarters (i.e. 10 years) was
eventually chosen in order to capture a consistent domain of historic economic
behavior.

A few (in the order of a dozen or so) top leading indicator candidates were
chosen through a combination of this screening method and business judgment.
Business judgment was critical in ensuring the relevance of the chosen leading
indicators as well as their domain. Three domain areas were deemed important:
(i) raw commodity prices; (ii) labor-related indices; and (iii) financial indicators.

These top choices were then divided into two separate groups of indicators, each
group containing representatives from all three domains of importance. Two neural

---

[52]The term "snippet" was coined to represent a time series of given length.

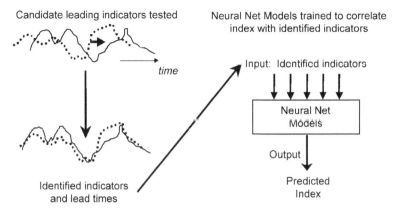

Figure 19.2.   Modeling approach.

net models were then trained on these two sets of indicators to develop a correlation between the drivers (which comprised the input to the nets) and the index of interest. The reason for so dividing the indicators and modeling them separately was that the agreement between the two models based on different drivers would increase the confidence in the predictions. Figure 19.2 schematically illustrates the overall approach.

19.3.   MODEL RESULTS

As mentioned earlier, two neural net models were constructed for forecasting the index. Each used different drivers as inputs, and the consistency between the results of these different nets was a measure of the confidence in their predictions. The drivers for each model were distributed so as to represent a mix of commodity, labor-related, and financial indicators.

To ensure robust predictive capability, these nets were trained on 40 quarters of data, tested for predicting the index for the last 5 quarters for which data were available, and then queried for projecting the index over 5 additional quarters. In all cases, the lead-time between the leading drivers and the cost index was at least 5 quarters so that the index could be forecasted for slightly more than 1 year ahead of currently available information.

Neural net Model I was trained using four input drivers: two of which were commodity indices; one a labor-related index; and one a financial index. Five input drivers were used for Model II: two being commodity indices; two being financial indices; and one a labor-related index. Figures 19.3 and 19.4 show the results of

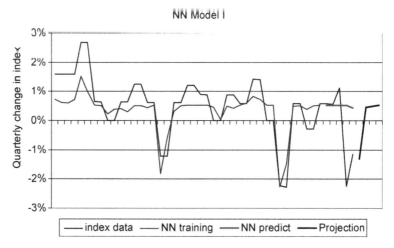

Figure 19.3. Results for Model I—quarterly change of index vs. time.

these two models. In these figures the quarterly change in the index is plotted on the ordinate vs. time (in quarters) on the abscissa. The different colored lines indicate the actual data for the index, how well the models learned the data on which they were trained, and how they predicted the index. The red line shows model predictions of the index over 5 quarters where index data were available; the heavy brown line indicates projections of the index into the future. The predictive consistency between the two models is the key factor in inspiring confidence in them. It is interesting to observe that both models predicted the sharp change in the index and both caught the change 2 quarters after it occurred.

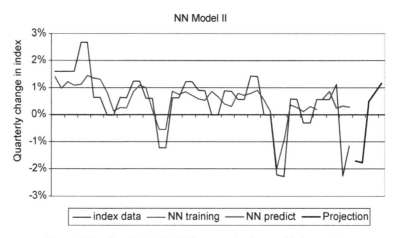

Figure 19.4. Results for Model II—quarterly change of index vs. time.

19.4.   CONCLUSIONS

With the model predicting the change in the index value for each quarter, a time series showing the transacted price index forecast can be constructed.

This two-pronged approach can be used for: (1) identifying whether an indicator leads the industry-specific variable of interest and, if so, the leading time interval; (2) developing forecasting models for any industry-specific variable where historical data are available.

A high level of confidence in such forecasts is critically important. This is realized by constructing multiple models using different leading indicators and relying on their predictions only when these different models give similar results.

Chapter 20
Corporate Demographic Trend Analysis

20.1. BACKGROUND

A major corporation became concerned about possible gender-related pay bias within their organization. They wanted to rapidly determine whether their concerns were valid and, if so, to what extent (quantitatively) were there salary differences between similarly qualified individuals of different genders.

20.2. ISSUES

The company's several acquisitions had resulted in a profusion of disparate job titles and functional roles. While the salary grades within the company were distinct and well defined, employees within each grade had varying levels of education, job titles, responsibility, ages, lengths of service, and years in their current positions, etc. The challenge was to extract reliable gender-related salary patterns from multiple confounding other factors mentioned above.

20.3. APPROACH AND MODEL CONFIGURATION

The first step in discovering underlying trends by mining the corporate salary/demographic data available for a particular calendar year involved identifying common job functionalities associated with the various job titles. For a variety of reasons there were approximately 800 different job titles distributed within the 2000 employee pool for which data were provided. Left in this form the data would have posed considerable modeling difficulties on account of the disproportionately large number of degrees of freedom compared to the total number of data. Text-based clustering analysis performed on the job titles resulted in the 800 or so job titles being organized into just 17 distinct functional categories, thereby making the problem far more amenable to robust modeling.

Several gender-blind models (see Figure 20.1) were then created to correlate salaries with the following demographic properties:

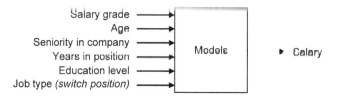

Figure 20.1. Model configuration.

- Salary grade
- Age
- Years with the company (i.e. seniority)
- Years in present job position
- Education level
- Job type/function (one of 17 switch positions)

The idea behind creating gender-blind models which learned to associate salary with other characteristics was that these associations could then be compared with the actual salaries, so uncovering any bias that might be gender related. Deviations of actual salaries from model results were averaged separately for the different genders over each salary grade.

20.4.   MODEL RESULTS AND CONCLUSIONS

Several neural net models, with different degrees of freedom[53] and seeds for initiating the nets' weights, were trained on the data to ensure that the patterns and trends extracted were consistent for all the models. For each individual, the difference between the actual salary and the salary learned by the gender-blind models was calculated. Then, within each salary grade, these differences were averaged for each gender. Had there been no gender bias, these averages would have been close to zero. However, it turned out that this was not the case. There was a significant gender bias against females for all salary grades except for the highest one. There were, however, very few females in the highest salary grade (only 4%), and so the results for this grade were not reliable.

These results are shown in Figures 20.2 and 20.3 based on four models, coded wJ1 through wJ4. The results of the four models are very similar.

---

[53]i.e. different number of hidden layer neurons.

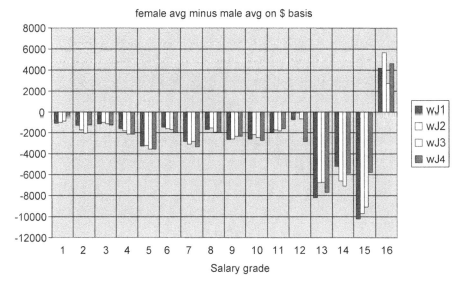

Figure 20.2. Models showing gender differential on a dollar basis.

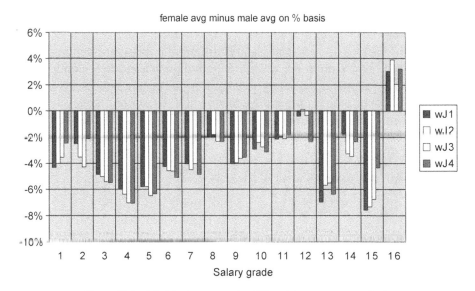

Figure 20.3. Models showing gender differential on a percentage basis.

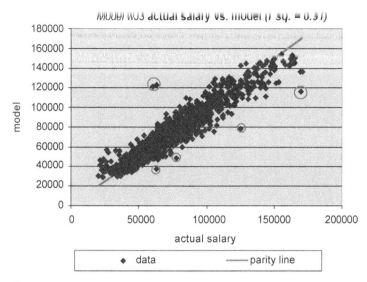

Figure 20.4. Parity plot of model results versus actual salary for each individual.

Figure 20.2 shows the average differential results on a dollar basis for each salary grade. These results are also shown on a percentage basis in Figure 20.3.

It is worth examining the extent to which the models learned to correlate salaries from the data. As all the models' results were quite similar, Figure 20.4 shows a parity plot for one of the models. All six outliers (circled in red) were identified by each of the four models, and were presented to the client for further investigation.

Table 20.1 shows the overall salary differential between genders in the employee pool. This pattern recognition-based approach enabled identifying the effects of gender alone in the salary treatment of all the employees. Its power in taking into account other confounding factors and extracting the key feature of interest is amply demonstrated in this case study. As a result of studies such as this, it is possible to detect and correct biases in systems and organizations.

Table 20.1. Overall salary gender differential in the employee pool

| Model | Overall female Δ | | Model | Actual | Model |
	$	%	avg. $	avg. $	r^2
wJ1	− $2293	− 3.99%	$67,652	$67,835	0.91
wJ4	− $2448	− 4.47%	$67,855	$67,835	0.91
wJ3	− $2331	− 4.32%	$67,896	$67,835	0.91
wJ2	− $2152	− 4.03%	$67,901	$67,835	0.91

Epilogue[†]

A century or so ago most people traveled on horseback while only a few very affluent individuals had cars. Today, most of us ride in cars whereas only the very well-off can afford to have horses! Way back then, most homes were poorly lit by oil lamps while dazzling incandescent electric lights illuminated only the homes of the rich. Today, all of us have access to bright electric lighting; one has to pay quite extravagantly for a meal in a dim, candle-lit restaurant!

Up until now, considerable resources and high-powered technical talent are captive to the formulation and number crunching procedures necessary for the development of process and business models, leaving little technical horsepower in reserve for exploring fantasies that our imaginations generate. We hope that this book will lead to an inversion in industry's technical expectation and capability so that as pattern recognition technology allows us to build models rapidly and cost-effectively directly from operating data, technical talent and resources can be freed up to dream of and realize game-changing new and profitable technical and business opportunities.

[†]The sentiment in the first paragraph of this epilogue was encountered by the author several years ago. Unfortunately the author is unable to locate the source.

Appendices

Appendix A1
Thermodynamics and Information Theory

A1.1. THERMODYNAMIC CONCEPTS SET THE STAGE FOR QUANTIFYING INFORMATION

The foundation on which thermodynamics is based makes its postulates very generally applicable. The First Law, which deals with energy conservation, can be restated in its essence as: "One cannot give that which one does not have". The implications of this should be a required study for all aspiring politicians. The Second Law deals with the direction of time's arrow, prescribing how systems behave naturally. For instance, a cup of hot tea, once poured, will always cool down until it is at room temperature, and will never reheat itself spontaneously. The tea cooling down is an irreversible process. Scrambling an egg is another such irreversible process, as it is impossible to unscramble it and return the universe[54] to its pristine state.[55]

Exposure to the core principles of thermodynamics facilitates the understanding of information theory. Hence, we shall devote the next sections to a few basic definitions and thermodynamic explanations.

A *system* is an item or a collection of items of fixed identity upon which attention is focused for study. The *state* of a system is the condition in which it exists, and is described by a set of *properties* that govern the system's behavior [1].

A can of soda is an example of a physical system, the state of which can be described by the mass and composition of its contents, its temperature, and its internal pressure. An equities market comprised of the stocks of certain companies (excluding, for the time being, any transfer of money or stock across the market's boundary) could be considered as an example of a financial system. The market prices and underlying fundamentals of the constituent equities describe its state. A financier may take objection to this by saying that the state is also governed by its *surroundings*, including the psychology of the traders that operate in the market,

---

[54]The universe consists of the hen, the egg, and the surroundings.

[55]A wit once remonstrated against this observation, claiming that feeding the scrambled egg to a hen, which would then lay an unscrambled egg, would reverse the scrambling. A sounder understanding of thermodynamics than that possessed by the wit would, however, lead to appreciating the fact that the processes undertaken by the hen while laying the egg (such as metabolic digestion, respiration, transferring heat to the surroundings, flapping its wings, clucking, mating, etc.) irreversibly change the universe.

and other economic conditions. However, while the traders may exert forces that could change the state of the system, the state itself is indeed defined at any given moment by the properties we have mentioned. Such a state might be unstable, subject to spontaneous change if the forces acting on the system were not balanced. On the other hand, if all the forces acting on the system balanced each other, the system would be in *equilibrium* with its surroundings, and would remain unchanged as long as the balanced forces acting on it did not change. The state of a system will not spontaneously change as long as the system is in *equilibrium* with its surroundings. A *process* is defined as the path taken by a system as it moves from one state to another.

Work is defined as exerting a force over some finite distance. The effective result of the process of doing work could be the lifting of a weight. For example, the flow of an electric current can result in (but is not necessarily limited to) the lifting of a weight when passed through an electric motor. This definition of work can be extended to any useful endeavor leading to the commandeering of resources which could (if so directed) lead to the lifting of a weight.

The implication of this definition is that in order to obtain work from a system, the system must move from one state to another, i.e. undergo a process of some sort. A new term, the *availability* of a system, now needs to be introduced for describing a system's potential to do useful work. A system's availability depends on how far the state of the system is from equilibrium with its surroundings. A system in equilibrium can do no useful work, and so has zero availability. The farther a system is from its equilibrium state, the greater is its availability, its potential to do useful work, and the potential profit one can derive from it.

A1.2. EQUILIBRIUM AS A STATE OF DISORDER — ORGANIZATION AS A VALUE-ADDING PROCESS

One of the laws of nature (the Second Law of Thermodynamics) dictates that systems become disordered with time, moving towards an eventual state of rest or equilibrium unless an external force is exerted on them to prevent this motion. For example, left to its own accord, a room will become progressively more "dusty". Dust will settle randomly all over the room's surfaces. The process of "dusting" a room results in increasing the order of the dust (or rather, decreasing the disorder of the dust) so that at the end of the process the dust is confined to a small, designated space (i.e. a dustbin). To reduce the dust's disorder we would have to do work *on* the system (or on the dust, in this case).[56] We are never likely to observe a spontaneous process in which randomly distributed dust organizes itself into a dustbin. Therefore, the probability of finding a system in a disordered state is greater than that of finding one in an ordered state. A maximally disordered state, comprising of dust spread randomly everywhere within the room, is one of equilibrium that the system naturally evolves towards. Hence, an equilibrium state is the most probable one in which we would expect to find a system.

Summing up, an equilibrium state corresponds to one of random distribution within a system and is the most probable state for a given system. Systems at equilibrium have low intrinsic value. Work would have to be done on these systems in order to organize them, and by so doing enhance their value.

A1.3. ENTROPY, DISORDER, AND UNCERTAINTY

In our previous example, we saw that an equilibrium state corresponds to one of disorder in which dust is scattered randomly over a room's surfaces. Let us compare this state to an ordered one in which all the dust particles were swept up and collected in a dustbin. In the latter case, there would be little uncertainty about where a particular dust particle could be found in the room; the answer would be: "in the dustbin". In contrast to this, for a system at equilibrium, there is a great deal of uncertainty regarding where exactly any particular dust particle could be found in the room. The most probable state is that in which there is the greatest amount of uncertainty about the system.

Entropy is a thermodynamic property quantifying the extent of disorder in a system. On a microscopic[57] scale we express this property mathematically in the following way:

$$S \approx \ln w \tag{A1.1}$$

where S is the entropy of the system and w the number of possible locations of finding any particular dust particle.

If the room is totally ordered, or perfectly cleaned, so that all the dust resides in an extremely small dustbin, then there is only one possible location for any particular dust particle, and the entropy is zero. On the other hand, the entropy

---

[56]In order to expend the energy to do this work we will increase the disorder in the environment: by converting ordered matter (food) into disordered matter (excretion) [2]. The Second Law dictates that the amount of order created by collecting the dust is less than the amount of disorder resulting from the equivalent conversion of food to excretion. Hence, the net disorder in the universe will increase as a result of our effort in cleaning the room.

[57]As opposed to a macroscopic scale.

of a highly disordered system is very large. Entropy, therefore, is a measure of the degree of uncertainty about a system.

Entropy also gives us a measure of the quality of energy present in a system. Another law of nature (the First Law of Thermodynamics)[58] states that energy is conserved: it can neither be created nor destroyed. If that is the case, why should we ever be concerned about an "energy crisis" in which we "run out of energy"? This seeming paradox is resolved by appreciating that such a crisis pertains not to energy per se, but to *available* energy. As we mentioned earlier, we need an available potential difference to exploit in order to extract useful energy or work. The lower the entropy of any system, the greater is its potential to do useful work. As we will see later, because of the relationships between entropy, disorder, and uncertainty, the quantification of information (which is connected with uncertainty) is built upon the foundations laid by thermodynamics in conceptualizing entropy.

A1.4. OPPORTUNITIES FOUND IN IMBALANCES

Opportunities lie in being able to identify and exploit imbalances in systems. Energy can be extracted from flowing water provided there is a difference in height between the surface levels of the water source and the sink. The extracted energy is the result of exploiting the gravitational potential difference (or imbalance) between the source and the sink. No gravitational energy can be extracted from a single pool of water, regardless of how high or low its surface level may be, as long as there is no access to another body of water at a different level. This is another manifestation of the Second Law of Thermodynamics. We hear about "energy crises" in the popular press. According to the First Law of Thermodynamics, energy can neither be created nor destroyed.[59] How then can we be "running out" of energy? This issue is resolved when we understand that it is not energy that we are "running out" of, but the quality of energy that is being degraded, thereby making less of the existing energy useable. We receive highly ordered energy from the sun; use this to drive our engines and motor our activities, the irreversible nature of which degrades the energy; and eventually send the energy back into the universe as relatively disordered thermal radiation.[60]

---

[58]Though neither the First nor the Second Law of Thermodynamics has ever been proven, their violation has never been observed.

[59]In the absence of nuclear reactions.

[60]The quality of radiated energy is related to the temperature of the radiation source: the higher the temperature, the higher the quality of the radiated energy. Radiation received from the sun originates at the solar surface temperature; the thermal radiation of our waste heat to the rest of the Universe is emitted at the Earth's (much lower) surface temperature.

Another physical example of extracting energy to do useful work by exploiting an imbalance is the combustion of fuel in an engine. The unburned fuel has a higher level of potential chemical energy than the potential chemical energy level of the resulting products of combustion. Similarly, in financial systems, imbalances between two or more states offer arbitrage opportunities, e.g. differences in the price of a commodity at different locations or the potential for changes in price at different instances of time.

A1.5.   APPRECIATION THROUGH QUANTIFICATION

Measuring something is one of the first steps in being able to know it. To what extent does the appreciation of something require it to be quantifiable? How can the information contained in a document or transferred in a message be quantified? Earlier sections in this appendix discussed qualitative differences between ordered and disorganized systems. These differences will now be quantified.

A1.6.   QUANTIFYING INFORMATION TRANSFER

Consider the transmission of a message regarding the outcome of a certain event [3,4]. Suppose there were P_o equally likely possible outcomes for an event, and the receiver had no prior knowledge of the actual outcome conveyed in the message. We define the level of uncertainty U_i of the receiver prior to the message's transmission as

$$U_i = K \ln(P_o) \tag{A1.2}$$

where K is some constant of proportionality. Note the similarity between this expression and that for entropy in Eq. (A1.1).

Were there to be no ambiguity in the transmission and reception of the message, there is only one realized outcome. The uncertainty U_f upon receiving such a message is

$$U_f = K \ln(1) = 0 \tag{A1.3}$$

The amount of information I transferred by this message is the difference between the uncertainty levels before and after the message was received

$$I = U_i - U_f = K \ln(P_o) \tag{A1.4}$$

Had there been some ambiguity in the transmission or reception of the message, a finite number of possible outcomes, P_f, after the message was received would depend on the extent of unresolved uncertainty. P_f would range in value between unity (no ambiguity) and P_o (no resolution of the signal in the message). The information transferred would then be

$$I = U_i - U_f = K \ln(P_o/P_f) \tag{A1.5}$$

where $1 \leq P_f \leq P_o$.

A property can be meaningfully quantified only if it is associated with a unit of measure. For example, if the distance between two locations is 2 km (kilometer) the qualifier *km* gives meaning to the numerical value 2. If centimeter (cm) were used as the unit of measure, the same distance would have a value of 200,000 cm. Just the numbers "2" or "200,000" by themselves do not have any significance in describing distance. Units of measure therefore need to be ascribed for quantifying information and uncertainty.

Bits are used as units in the computer world to specify amounts of data. A *bit*[61] is a binary unit of measure (having a value of either 0 or 1) and is derived from "binary digit". In the previous example, were the message to consist of x bits, then P_o is equal to 2^x (as each bit has two possible outcomes). If no ambiguity is associated with the transmission and reception of the message, Eq. (A1.4) becomes [3]:

$$I = Kx \ln(2) \tag{A1.6}$$

As the length of message I is x bits, the constant K can be evaluated:

$$I = x = Kx \ln(2)$$

$$\therefore K = 1/\ln(2) \tag{A1.7}$$

A1.7. INFORMATION CONTENT IN A SYSTEM

The expressions describing changes in uncertainty and entropy are similar. Making use of entropy as a system property will therefore help express the information content of a system. Three major issues need to be addressed. (1) The value of entropy moves synchronously with uncertainty, and therefore in the opposite direction of information content. (2) The units of entropy derived from thermodynamic convention[62] will need to be reconciled with those required

---

[61]In his seminal 1948 paper on information theory [5] Shannon cited J. W. Tukey as having suggested the term *bit*.

[62]Energy per degree of temperature.

for expressing information content. (3) It should be emphasized that our attempts at quantifying information have not yet addressed the *value* of information from a viewpoint of its usefulness; rather, they have dealt only with the uncertainty of outcomes expressed in the form of the number of possible options.

A1.7.1 Negentropy

Useful work was defined as that which could result in raising a weight. The "quality" of energy was an important factor in determining how usefully energy could be harnessed. For instance, mechanical energy (e.g. in the form of a compressed spring) can be directly converted to raising a weight, and consequently can be said to be energy of a very high quality. On the other hand, thermal energy (in the form of a temperature difference between two bodies) can, at best, be only partially converted to raising a weight because of Carnot's principle.[63] At worst, it can be entirely unutilized if the heat flows untapped from the hot to the cold body. The concept of entropy in a *negative sense* leads towards determining the potential of a system to do useful work; hence we introduce the term *negentropy*. The higher the negentropy of a system, the greater its potential to do useful work, and the greater its information content.

A1.7.2 Units of Entropy

Classical thermodynamics defines the change in entropy of a system as the heat transferred reversibly[64] to it divided by the system's temperature. The unit of entropy, therefore, is energy per degree of temperature. The microscopic view of the entropy of a system (Eq. (A1.1)) corresponding to these units becomes

$$S = k \ln(w) \qquad (A1.8)$$

where k is the Boltzmann constant (1.38×10^{-23} J/K) and w the number of microstates corresponding to the macrostate describing the system.[65]

---

[63]Carnot's principle specifies the maximum amount of work obtainable by operating an engine between two reservoirs at specified temperatures. Nature thus imposes limits on the efficiencies we can expect from the engines we use to drive our appliances and conveyances.

[64]The seemingly contradictory idea of "reversible heat transfer" is dealt with in more detail in classical thermodynamic texts, e.g., [1]. In short, a reversible process is one which, when reversed, returns both the system and its surroundings to the original state they were in prior to the process. In real life no process is truly reversible as entropy inevitably increases as a consequence of any activity. However, an idealized reversible (or quasi-equilibrium) process can be approached if it were performed in infinitesimally small steps over an infinitely long time interval.

[65]A microstate of a system is the exact specification of the constituents and configuration of the system. A macrostate is the ensemble of different microstates each of which exhibit the same macroscopic system property Ref. [4].

A1.7.3 Value of Information

We will break fresh and potentially controversial ground by attempting to assign value to information, rather than stopping at merely quantifying the extent of uncertainty or ambiguity. We do so by invoking the concept of availability, which addresses the potential for doing useful work. Information exchange has been expressed as a change in uncertainty, which in turn is directly related to negentropy.

The thermodynamic availability of a system is expressed as the maximum work that the system is capable of doing by undergoing a reversible process in moving to equilibrium from its existing state. If the system's volume does not change, then

$$\text{Availability} = \Delta U - T\Delta S \qquad (A1.9)$$

where ΔU is the difference in energy between the existing state and equilibrium, T the system temperature, and ΔS the entropy difference between the existing state and equilibrium.

The analog of this expression as it pertains to the information content of a system is

$\Delta U = \{$(energy available through arbitrage opportunity derived from information) $-$ (energy required to transmit and receive the information)$\}$

$T(-\Delta S) =$ energy corresponding to the reduction in uncertainty through obtaining the information

Information theory has addressed the meaning and derivation of the $T(-\Delta S)$ term. The ΔU term embodies the energy available through arbitrage opportunity derived from information as an increment over a pre-existing reference (or base) state of knowledge.

REFERENCES

[1] Van Wylen, G.J. & Sonntag, R.E. (1976) *Fundamentals of Classical Thermodynamics*, 2nd Edition, Wiley, New York.

[2] Schroedinger, E. (1967) *What is Life?*, Cambridge University Press, Cambridge, Reprint.

[3] Brillouin, L. (1962) *Science and Information Theory*, 2nd Edition, Academic Press, London.

[4] Sonntag, R.E. & Van Wylen, G.J. (1966) *Fundamentals of Statistical Thermodynamics*, Wiley, New York.

[5] Shannon, C.E. (1948) A mathematical theory of communication. *Bell Syst. Tech. J.*, **27** (3), July.

Appendix A2
Modeling

A2.1. WHAT ARE MODELS

As mentioned earlier, models are abstractions of reality. Their purpose is to explain and predict physical, economic, or social phenomena. We relate to our environment through models. Whereas scientists and engineers use systematic mathematical formulation to build models, every human being, consciously or (most often) subconsciously, develops internalized models based on experience to yield expectations for interactions with the external world. Though any model that we are capable of building is too simplified to portray reality completely, skillfully built models can adequately explain and predict real phenomena that do not deviate too far from the domain for which they were developed. A model's merit is determined by how closely its results correspond to actual observations and over how wide a range it is valid. It is critical that a model's user be cognizant of the domain and conditions for which a particular model yields valid results.

Developing a model for an industrial application could be viewed analogously to conducting an orchestral symphonic movement: ideally, the conductor's upbeat initiating the exposition should embody within it the final resolution of the movement's coda. Sonata form, comprising of exposition, development, recapitulation, and coda, has its counterpoint in modeling: problem formulation (exposition); algorithm development (development); validation (recapitulation); interpretation and fruition of deployment (coda).

A2.2. MECHANISTIC MODELING — GENERAL LAWS

The earliest mathematical[66] models were inspired by the desire to express natural observations of causes and effects succinctly. Newton's famous law of motion implies[67] an expression relating the acceleration, a, caused by a force, F, acting on

---

[66]Mathematics may be viewed as a language devised for precise and concise expression of scientific ideas. The field of pure mathematics may be considered as the province of mathematical linguists and poets; and applied mathematicians, engineers, and working scientists viewed as users of mathematical prose. Just as natural languages can be used either eloquently (as in great literature or rhetoric) or clumsily, mathematical expression can range in its degree of elegance.

[67]Under the circumstance of the body's mass remaining constant.

a body of mass m

$$F = ma \qquad (A2.1)$$

Axioms such as this are stated rather than proven, with the expectation that they may lead to deriving models for explaining physical phenomena.[68] Eq. (A2.1) explains much about the motion of objects in our world provided that relativistic and quantum mechanical effects do not predominate. Other examples of models based on observations establishing mechanistic principles are the laws of thermodynamics, a few of which we discussed earlier.

Laws of this type form a body of fundamental knowledge having wide applicability. Despite their generality, their conception was informed by observations[69] and, in many cases, experiments. Therefore, by definition[70] these laws have empirical roots.

A2.3. PARTICULAR LAWS AND CONSTITUTIVE RELATIONS

Less general models developed from the observed behavior of particular systems are no less useful than those based on general laws. For example, the flow of electric current is described by Ohm's law which relates the current I flowing through a body to the applied voltage V and a material property of the body, i.e. its resistance R

$$V = IR \qquad (A2.2)$$

The conductive flow of heat through a body is described by Fourier's law of heat conduction, which also relates the flow (heat flux in this case) to the driving force (temperature difference) through a material property of the body (thermal conductivity). Thus

$$\dot{q}'' = k \cdot \nabla T \qquad (A2.3)$$

where $\dot{q}''$ is the heat flux (i.e. rate of heat flow per unit area), T the temperature, and k the thermal conductivity of the body.

Yet another example, the rate at which the temperature of a body can be increased (or decreased), is expressed in terms of the rate at which heat flows into (or out of) the body and the body's heat capacity C

$$\dot{q} = mC\dot{T} \qquad (A2.4)$$

---

[68]Private communication with William B. Heard.

[69]Private communications with William B. Heard and Robert M. Koros.

[70]**Empirical**, *adj.* (of knowledge) based on observation or experiment, not on theory—*definition in the Oxford American Dictionary, Oxford University Press, 1980.*

where $\dot{q}$ is the rate of heat flow, $\dot{T}$ the rate change of temperature, m the body's mass, and C the body's heat capacity.

These models serve as definitions of material properties in order to describe the behavior of particular flows, and are also called constitutive relations. The material properties need not have constant values. They may well depend on system conditions. For example, the heat capacity C may be a function of temperature T in order that the model in Eq. (A2.4) portrays observed behavior more accurately.

A2.4. COMBINING GENERAL LAWS AND CONSTITUTIVE RELATIONS

Combining general laws with constitutive relations for particular systems result in the creation of very useful models. Examples of this include the Navier–Stokes equations [1] describing the motion of fluids. These equations invoke a general principle of momentum conservation (which follows from Newton's laws of motion) in order to delineate and quantify the forces acting on a fluid. Constitutive relations defining viscosity, a property of the fluid, are incorporated into the Navier–Stokes equations to model the shear (or rubbing) forces between fluid elements.

A2.5. MODELING DIRECTLY FROM DATA

Technical and business fronts are advancing at ever increasing rates. This accelerating pace of progress puts increasing demands on being able to assimilate very quickly all that is happening. Not only is the number of new processes to be modeled increasing but also the levels of detail and complexity that need to be captured by predictive models in order to satisfy market forces are also increasing. Formulating conventional models is becoming progressively more expensive in time and effort. Competitive advantage is gained by developing robust models (automatically, if possible) directly from operating experience, i.e. data, and then optimizing their results to provide effective strategies and decisions.

REFERENCE

[1] Sabersky, R. & Acosta, A. (1964) *Fluid Flow*, Macmillan, New York.

Index

a priori mechanistic models 64–6
absolute causal indices 70
activity profiles 77–8
adaptive learning 7–8
  biological neural networks 17–25
  business applications 107–9
  coupled genetic algorithms 106
  process industry application modes
    103–7
  reactor modeling 111–18
adaptive learning reactor models
  (ALRM) 114–15
ALRM *see* adaptive learning reactor
  models
appendices 163–73
  information theory 163–70
  modeling 171–3
  thermodynamics 163–70
artificial neural nets 18
author activity profiles 77–8
auto-clustering 49–56, 68–9, 107
autoclassification 13, 51–5, 76–7
availability of systems 164, 166, 170
axioms 172

back-propagation (backprops) neural nets
  constraints 65–6
  feedforward neural nets 33–6
  general transformation functions 37–9
  mixed data type incorporation 67
  pre-conditioning data 42–4
  sigmoidal functions 35–6, 39, 42–4
  supervised learning 19–21, 33–44
  training 36–7
  weights 36–41
bi-level focusing 143–7
bias 108, 137, 155–8
binary data distances 11
binary genes 89

binary switches 90
bins 18
biological principle methods 5, 17–25
bits 11, 168
breeding 96–8, 106

capital investment strategies 149–53
Carnot's principle 169
Cartesian distances 45–46
case studies
  catalyst deactivation 111–18
  coking in fired heaters 123–6
  demographic bias 155–6
  distillation tower temperatures 137–41
  forecasting price changes 149–53
  fouling predictions 123–6
  gender-related pay bias 155–6
  operation credits 127–30
  pilot plant scale-ups 131–6
  plant stack emissions 119–22
  price change forecasts 149–53
  process design enablement 143–7
  profitability 103–10
  reactor catalyst deactivation 111–18
  tracer diagnostics 131–6
catalyst activity uncertainties 104–5
catalyst deactivation predictions 111–18
causal indices 70–2
cause and effect 149–53
center of gravity 13
centroids 13, 45
characterizing data 9–10
characterizing textual material 75–82
chemical plant runs 104–5
chromosomes 90–3, 96–8
classifying textual material 75–82
clusters
  activation 46–7
  autoclassifying documents 76–7

center seeding 44–5
distances 46, 50–1, 68–9
distillation tower temperatures 140–1
gender-related pay bias 155–8
organizing data 13, 22–4
radius 50–1
self-organizing data 22–4
signal separation from noise 41–2
coking in fired heaters 123–6
colors 12–13
commodity composite baskets 149–53
competitive advantages 117–18
competitive intelligence 109
competitive learning 51–6
composite basket of commodities 149–53
computational science 17–25
confidence levels 27, 67–9
conjugate gradient methodology 40–1
connection weights 36–9
constitutive relations 172–3
constraints 64–6
continuous variables 89–90
convergence 40–1, 45
corporate demographic trend analysis
    155–8
correlation
    organizing data 14–15
    price change forecasting 149
    radial basis function 47
    supervised learning 21–4, 33–48
cosine between vectors 53–4, 75–8, 83–4
coupled genetic algorithms 98–100, 106,
    132–6
credit risk predictions 108, 127–30
cross-over 93–5
cross-validation 41–2, 121–2
customization 7–8, 57–73

data
    characterization 9–10
    distances 11–13
    knowledge and information 3
    mining 137–41, 155

pattern classification 21–2
patterns 9–15
pre-conditioning 27–8, 42–4, 47, 55–6
series resonance 14
space points 46–7
types 9, 66–7
data-driven modeling 7–8
    coupled genetic algorithms 106
    customization 57–73
    extrapolation 58–64
    hybrid combinations 62–4
daughters 93–5
decoking 123–6
degree of confidence 27, 67–9
degree of resonance 83–7
degrees of freedom 156
delta rule 36–7
demographic data bias 108, 155–8
digital data distances 12–13
digital variables 66–7
discrete data distances 12–13
discrete switches 90
disorder 164–6
distances 11–13, 45–6, 50–1, 68–9
distillation tower temperatures 137–41
document classification/characterization
    75–82, 155–8
dollar basis gender-related pay bias 156–8
dot product 53–4, 75–8, 83–4
drivers 83–7, 149–53

embedding idealized models 58–64
embedding a priori mechanistic
    understanding 64–6
emission predictions 104, 119–22
empirical modeling issues 27–30, 57–8
employee pools 158
energy 163–70
entropy 5–6, 79–82, 163–6, 168–70
environment assessment 108–9
environmental emissions 104, 119–22
equation of state 58
equilibrium, disorder 164–5

Printed and bound by CPI Group (UK) Ltd, Croydon, CR0 4YY

03/10/2024

01040415-0020

Euclidean distance 11–12
exactness 57–8
experimental judgement 28–9
expert systems 18
extrapolation 27–9, 58–64, 147

feed characteristics 105, 113, 119–20,
    123–4
feedforward neural nets 33–6
field deployment 117
fingerprinting 75–8, 109
fired pipestill heaters 123–6
First Law of Thermodynamics 5, 163,
    166–7
fit solutions 106
fitness of chromosomes 90–1
floating point numbers 66, 90
flow regimes 127–36
fluidized bed reactors 131–6
food industry 143–7
forecasting 86–7, 149–53
fouling predictions 123–6
Fourier's law of heat transfer 172
Freon-12 58–64

GAs *see* genetic algorithms
Gaussian functions 24, 46–7
gender-related pay bias 155–8
general transformation functions 37–9
genes 90
genetic algorithms (GAs) 89–100
    breeding 106
    coupling 98–100, 106, 132–6
    definitions 90
    introduction 7–8
    mating 93–8
    mutation 94–8
    natural selection principles 24–5
    product formulation 98–100
    profitable operating strategies 98
    simulation model coupling 132–6
genetic natural selection 17, 24–5
graphical interpretation 72–3

Hamming distance 11
heat capacity 172–3
heat transfer 29, 172
Hoerl functions 81–2
Holland, John 89, 96
hybrid combinations 62–4
hydrocarbons 123–6
hydrodynamic models 131–6
hydroprocessing reactors 111–18

ideal gas (IG) model 58–64
IG *see* ideal gas
imbalances, opportunities in 166–7
in situ adaptive learning 104–5, 111–18
index value changes 149–53
industrial strength applications 57–73
industry-specific variables 149–53
information
    content 168–70
    knowledge and data 3
    rich word skimming 80–1
    theory 4–6, 163–70
input data space seeding 44–5
interest factors 149–53
interpreting trained neural nets 69–73
introspection 6–7
inventor activity profiles 77–8
inverted process models 104
investment strategies 149–53

jack-knifing 41–2, 121–2
job titles and functions 155–8

keyword identification 79–82
knowledge 3

laboratory data enabled process
    design 143–7
laws
    constitutive relations 172–3
    law of heat transfer 172
    law of motion 171–2
    mechanistic modeling 171–2

leading indices 83–7, 149–53
learning error minimization 36–7
learning organisms 17–18
learning rate 54
liquid-vapor properties 143–7
log-log entropy maps 81–2

maldistributions 127–30
mapping outcomes 47
marketing 107
mating 93–8
mechanistic models 171–2
    embedding 58–64
    empiricism 28–9, 57–8
    hybrid combinations 62–4
microstates 169–70
mined data 137–41, 155
mixed data type incorporation 66–7
modeling 4–7
    aims 57
    appendices 171–3
    observation 6–7
    predictive empirical issues 27–30,
        57–8
molar volumes 58–61
momentum factor 40–1
monitoring 103–4
monomers 143–7
multi-position switches 90, 94
mutation algorithms 94–8

natural selection principles 24–5, 89
nearest neighbour 50–1
negentropy 169–70
neural nets 7–8
    see also back-propagation; Radial Basis
        Function; training...
    adaptive learning 17–25
    adaptive learning systems 18
    coupled genetic algorithms 98–100
    data-driven modeling 58–64
    interpretation 69–73
    learning organisms 17–18

organizing data patterns 13
price change forecasting 150–3
reactor catalyst deactivation predictions
    111–18
supervised learning 19–24, 33–48
time series analysis 83–7
unsupervised learning 18, 21–2
neuron transformation function 33–9
Newton's law of motion 171–2
next generation selection 92–3
noise 41–2, 127
nominal variables 9, 67
numerical data distances 11–12

observation, modeling 6–7
Ohm's law 172
operating characteristics 137–41, 143
operational credit predictions 127–30
optimizing algorithms 17, 24–5
order, thermodynamics 5–6
ordinal variables 9, 66–7
organizing data
    autoclassification 13
    clustering 13
    correlative modeling 14–15
    data series resonance 14
over-fitting 41–2

parents 93–4
parity plots 60–1, 63–4
particulate emissions 119–22
partition coefficients 143–7
percentage basis gender-related pay bias
    156–8
performance prediction 103–4
petroleum plant runs 104–5
pilot plants 106, 131–6
plants
    analysis 106, 131–6
    environmental
        emissions 104, 119–22
    monitoring 103–4
    stack emission predictions 119–22

staff 117
polymer products 143–7
populations 90–1
post-processing 27–8, 44
Prandtl number 29
pre-conditioning data 27–8, 42–4, 47, 55–6
pre-processing 27–8
predictive modeling
 back-propagation neural nets 33–6
 catalyst deactivation 111–18
 confidence measures 67–9
 credit risk 108, 127–30
 distillation tower temperatures 137–41
 empirical issues 27–30, 57–8
 fouling predictions 123–6
 performance 103–4
 profitability 103–4, 122
 reactor catalyst deactivation 111–18
price change forecasting 149–53
probability, cross-over 93–4
process, definition 164
process design enablement 143–7
process industry application modes 103–7
product formulation 98–100
product quality 105
profitability 98, 103–10, 122
property characterization models 105

qualitative differences 166–7
quantification 167–8

Radial Basis Function (RBF) neural nets
 auto-clustering 49–51
 clustering 22–4, 49–51
 confidence measures 68–9
 hybrid models 62–4
 input data space seeding 44–5
 nominal digital variables 67
 plant stack emission predictions 121–2
 self-organizing data 22–4
 supervised learning 44–7
 unsupervised learning 49–51

radiated energy 166
radius of the sphere of influence 46
rapid convergence 40–1
RBF *see* Radial Basis Function
reactor modeling 111–18
reading automation processes 75–82
reagents 127–30
reboilers 137–41
refinery units 119–30
relative causal indices 70
residual polymers 143–7
resonance 14, 83–7, 150
Reynolds number 29
robustness 28–9, 40–1, 151
roulette wheels 92–3

salary differences 155–8
saturated Freon-12 58–64
scaling 131–6, 143–7
scanning textual material 75–82
Second Law of Thermodynamics 5–6, 163–7
seeding 44–5
selection, chromosomes 92–3
self-organizing systems 7–8
 competitive learning 51–6
 distillation tower temperature predictions 138–41
 pilot plant analysis 106
 unsupervised learning 21–4, 49–56
sensitivity 42–4
shutdown 123–6
sigmoids 19, 21, 35–6, 39, 42–4
signal separation 41–2
simulation model-genetic algorithm coupling 132–6
skimming keywords 80–2
snippets 84, 150
spheres of influence 23, 46
spot-lighted scaling 143–7
stack emission predictions 119–22
start-up idiosyncrasies 104–5
state of disorder 164–5

state of systems 163
sulfur content 119–20
supervised learning
  adaptive learning systems 19–21
  back-propagation neural nets 33–44
  correlation 21–4, 33–48
  radial basis function neural nets 44–7
surroundings, definition 163–4
switches 90, 94–5
synapses 17–18
system, definition 163

temperature 123–30, 137–41
textual material
  characterization 75–82
  classification 75–82
  clustering analysis 155–8
  distances 13
  document classification 75–82
thermodynamics 4–6, 79–82, 163–70
time series analysis 14, 83–7, 149–53
time's arrow 163
TMT *see* tube metal temperatures
top-skimming keywords 81–2
tracer diagnostics 131–6
training neural nets
  catalyst deactivation 113–17
  graphical interpretation 72–3
  interpretation 69–73
  signal separation from noise 41–2
  weight adjustments 36–7

transacted price indices 149–53
transformation functions 33–9
tray temperatures 137–41
tube metal temperatures (TMT) 123–6

uncertainty 104–5, 164–5
unit monitoring 103–4
unsupervised learning 18, 21–4, 49–56

validation 41–2, 115–17, 121–2
value-adding processes 164–5
vapor-liquid equilibrium surface 58
variables
  data patterns 9
  data types 66–7
  genetic algorithms 89–90
vectoring documents 75–8
vectors 10
vigilance criterion 53–4
visualizing document contents 78–9

weighted roulette wheels 92–3
weights
  adaptive learning systems 18
  back-propagation neural
    nets 20, 36–41
  competitive learning 52–5
  gender-related pay bias 156
  radial basis function neural nets 47
work 164–5, 170